Asheville-Buncombe
Technical Community College
Learning Resources Center
340 Victoria Road
Asheville, NC 28801

DISCARDED

AUG 4 2025

MALE MID-LIFE CRISIS

Psychological Dynamics, Theological Issues, and Pastoral Interventions

Justin K. Lim

University Press of America,® Inc.
Lanham • New York • Oxford

Copyright © 2000 by
University Press of America,® Inc.

4720 Boston Way
Lanham, Maryland 20706

12 Hid's Copse Rd.
Cumnor Hill, Oxford OX2 9JJ

All rights reserved
Printed in the United States of America
British Library Cataloging in Publication Information Available

Library of Congress Cataloging-in-Publication Data

Lim, Justin K.
Male mid-life crisis : psychological dynamics, theological issues,
and pastoral interventions / Justin K. Lim.
p. cm.
Includes bibliographical references and index.
1. Middle aged men—Religious life. 2. Midlife crisis. 3. Midlife crisis—Religious aspects—Christianity. 4. Middle aged men—Pastoral counseling of. I. Title
BV4579.5.L55 2000   261.8'34244—dc21   00—042596 CIP

ISBN 0-7618-1766-2 (cloth:alk. ppr)
ISBN 0-7618-1767-0 (pbk: alk. ppr.)

∞™ The paper used in this publication meets the minimum
requirements of American National Standard for Information
Sciences—Permanence of Paper for Printed Library Materials,
ANSI Z39.48—1984

Dedicated to all people who struggle
to be generative men.

Acknowledgments

This book is the result of a cooperative partnership and life journey with my wife and my son. Also, I am indebted to many people for the completion of this book. Without them, it could not have been accomplished. The faculty of the Chicago Theological Seminary and the University of Chicago have challenged, opened and reshaped my intellectual horizons and journey through theology and psychology. Also, I cannot help thanking Ed de St. Aubin, Don McAdams and Solomon Cytrynbaum at Northwestern University who instructed and challenged me in the field of psychology. I appreciate to the University of Chicago Press for the permission of using Paul Tillich's *Systematic Thelogy*. Above all, without God's shepherding for this journey, it could not have been published.

CONTENTS

Acknowledgments
Introduction..1

PART I
The Male Self at Mid-life: Psychodynamic Interpretations

Chapter 1: Carl G. Jung's Analytical Understanding of the Self
and Mid-life Crisis

    Understanding of the Human Psyche and Life Cycle.............7
    Personal Unconscious and Collective Unconscious.............10
    Mid-life Confrontation with the Unconscious......................15
    The Self and the Archetype Image of God...........................20
    Summary..28

Chapter 2: Erik H. Erikson's Psycho-social Understanding of the
Self-Identity in Mid-life

    Epigenesis Structure of Human Development.....................33
    Generativity at Mid-life: Self-Identity as Immortality.........39
    Generativity as Instinctive Drive..46
    Implicative Meaning of Stagnation at Mid-life:
    Self-Destruction..49
    Summary..54

Chapter 3: Daniel Levinson's Research and Theory on Male
Mid-life Crisis

    Life Cycle and Mid-life..59
    Mid-life Transition..60
    Four Tasks of Mid-life Individuation...................................62
    Young/Old Archetype: Mayor Polarity................................63

PART II
Paul Tillich and Theology of the Male Self at Mid-life

Chapter 4: Tillich's Theological Interpretation on the Self

Theological Interpretations on the Self.................................73

The Centered Self as the Image of God...............................74
The Self-Estrangement..76
*The Self-loss and the World-loss as the Loss of
Determining Self*..79

The Actualization of the Self: Ontological Polarities of
the Self..81

The Self-Integration and Its Ambiguities.............................82
The Self-Creativity and Its Ambiguities...............................84
The Self-Transcendence and Its Ambiguities.......................87

Theological Direction for Regeneration of the Self
at Mid-life..90

The Divine Spirit and Its Influence on the Self...................90
*Theological Understanding of New Being
as the Recovering the Centered Self*......................................93
Theological Implications of Healing for Mid-life Crisis.....97

Summary..99

PART III
Pastoral Implications and Interventions for Male Mid-life:
A Contemporary Challenge for Ministry

Chapter 5: A Critical Dialogue of Psychology and Theology on Male Mid-life Crisis

Mortality as Non-being and Immortality as Desiring
the Centered Self..108
The Archetypal Image of God as the Centered Self..........114
A Critical Dialogue for Renewing the Centered Self........122

Chapter 6: Conclusion: Pastoral Implications and Interventions for
    Male Mid-life Crisis

    Pastoral Analysis for Male Mid-life Crisis and
    its Implications..131
    Male Mid-life Crisis and Spirituality...............................133
    Conclusive Suggestions: Pastoral Counseling as
    Spiritual Direction for Recovering the Centered Self......137
    Summary..147

    Bibliography..151
    Index..163
    About the Author

Introduction

The Purpose of The Study

The term, mid-life or mid-life crisis, was rarely used early in this century, because it is based on the current expectation of a life span of around 75 years.[1] Based on this long life expectancy a new term "mid-life" has been formed; not only have many influential books on this topic been published since the 70's, but also both research studies and the media, as well as our experience, have convinced middle-aged persons that mid-life is a crucial moment among life stages.[2] So it has become common to cite age forty as a turning point, the time when we leave one stage of life behind and enter another.[3] Actually, a result of research on male mid-life crisis strongly indicates that most male mid-lifers have experienced a crisis. According to the research 80 percent of male mid-lifers have experienced a mid-life identity/crisis.[4] Of course the reasons why most male mid-lifers have experienced mid-life crisis are various. The *Dictionary of Pastoral Care* describes the various reasons for mid-life crisis as follows:

> Mid-life crisis happens when a person is forced to redefine in a short period of time his or personal identity and goals because of aging body, a growing awareness of death, an unsatisfying marriage, the realization of limited career achievements or opportunities, the illness or death of parents, or the emerging independence of children.[5]

What these various causes challenge male mid-lifers to do is to rethink the meaning, value, and identity of life. Moreover, although the term "mid-life" appeared in the mid 70's, some scholars insist that its root is deeply associated with all times and countries.[6] Why do males have crises in middle age and how it can be traced to all ages and countries? I cannot handle all of these numerous reasons which are as many as hairs. And it is not the purpose of this dissertation to do so. My purpose, entangled with curiosity, is to figure out psychologically and theologically why this type of challenge, reevaluating one's identity at mid-life, is supposed to happen so intensively in mid-life that the term becomes popular and implies that it is a crucial moment.

In this vein, this study is theoretical research and has three purposes. First, as I mentioned previously, I think that there is some basic reason which causes male mid-life crisis to occur. I want to explore the psychological cause in the perspective of psychology. Secondly, I intend to understand, dialogue with and analyze psychologically and theologically the psychological cause, which I define as the concepts of "generativity" and "new being" in mid-life, relation to the first goal of this dissertation. Thirdly, I will examine how pastoral care can effectively provide pastoral interventions to male mid-lifers, so that we may experience life as transformed beings: "generative men" or "new beings."

The Significance of the Study

The first contribution and significance of this study is to redefine male mid-life crisis in terms of a psychological and theological interpretation. In some ways, until now the term male mid-life crisis has been considered to mean pleasure-seeking or suffering. Of course this type of phenomenon can be one of the causes of male mid-life crisis, but as I explore the meaning of male mid-life I intend to explore the hidden psychological and theological meanings of it - seeking the encounter with the archetypal image of God. As if it is difficult to see the sun beyond dark clouds, we have seen and criticized the phenomena that appears on the stage of male mid-life crisis, but have not explored what is behind the curtain. Secondly, it is a unique study which dialogues between the concept of the archetypal image of God, generativity and the new being. The dialogue provides readers with abundant and correct understandings regarding the meaning of male mid-life.

The Organization of the Study

This book consists of three parts with six chapters. In part I, I divide the content of it into three categories; Carl G. Jung, Erik H. Erikson and Daniel Levinson. In this chapter I show each psychologist's peculiar theory on male mid-life and their commonality and difference. In part II, which consists of three chapters, I focus on Paul Tillich's theological understandings of the self and reflections about the archetypal image of God and ontological courage (root), the Spiritual Presence, and New Being. I try to show theological understanding about what I know about psychological understandings about male mid-life identity through the pioneers' works and contemporary theories. In order to understand the meaning of pastoral care and counseling, I need to comprehend the psychological theories in the perspective of theology. In chapter 5, I focus on a critical dialogue between psychology and theology. In chapter 6, based on psychological and theological understandings, I analyze the meanings of male mid-life identity, suggest pastoral implications and interventions for male mid-lifers.

(Notes)

1. Barbara M. Newman, "Mid-Life Development" in *Handbook of Developmental Psychology*, ed. Benjamin B. Wolman (Englewood Cliffs, New Jersey: Prentice Hall, 1982), 617.
2. Elliott Jaques, "The Mid-life Crisis," in *Forty* (Knoxville: The University of Tennessee Press, 1985), 21.
3. Marjorie Fiske, *Middle Age* (New York: Harper & Row, 1979), 4.

4. Daniel Levinson, et. al, *The Seasons of a Man's Life* (New York: Ballantine Books, 1978), 199.
5. *Dictionary of Pastoral Care and Counseling,* s. v. "Mid-life Persons."
6. Daniel Levinson, op. cit., 31.

PART I

The Male Self at Mid-life: Psychodynamic Interpretations

Chapter 1

Carl G. Jung's Analytical Understandings of the Self and Mid-life Crisis

Understanding of the Human Psyche and Life Cycle

As I mentioned in the introduction of this study, male mid-life crisis or identity has been considered a general phenomenon. In this general perspective, what I have researched about mid-life crisis is not about individual phenomena of mid-life, which are supposed to vary based on individuals' situations, but about what the main psychological cause is which makes male mid-lifers experience mid-life crisis. In this sense, my intention in this part is to determine what in Jung's perspective is the strongest cause of male mid-life crisis. Jung's analytical psychology explains how the human psyche and life cycle are deeply associated with the causes of male mid-life crisis.

> The one hundred and eighty degrees of the arc of life are divisible into four parts. The first quarter, lying to the east, is child - that state in which we are a problem for others, but are not yet conscious of any problems of our own. Conscious problems fill out the second and third quarter.[1]

Jung divides the life cycle into two main stages. In order to describe the first 2 years which he names the "presexual stage," Jung defines "consciousness." He insists that "consciousness" comes from "knowing."

Infants do not have consciousness and it does not make any difficulties for them. In other words, there are no obstacles without consciousness. In this perspective, Jung indicates that "knowing" is based on a consciousness function. This means that infants have only sporadic memory functions because their psyche functions do not work fully. Thus, even though they have some experiences in this stage, they cannot remember what happened in the early stage of infancy.

> It is a fact that in the early years of life there is no continuous memory; at the most there are islands of consciousness which are like single lamps or lighted objects in the far-flung darkness. But these islands of memory are not the same as those initial connections between psychic contents; they contain something more and something new. This something is that highly important series of related contents which constitutes the so-called ego.[2]

Children speak of themselves in the third person, because the ego is an object in their consciousness. Jung does not mention when children can speak in "I-ness." But if the ego-contents are filled with their energy, they can speak in the first person. Starting with this stage, they can have continuous memory.[3] But though children have their own "I-ness," they are not totally independent from their parents. Not until they become adolescent do they enter the stage of psychic birth. According to Jung, psychic birth takes place in conscious differentiation from parents with the eruption of sexual life during the puberty.[4] In this stage youth show some peculiar phenomena. In the period of youth they put an end to the dreams of childhood, and prepare themselves to enter the professional world. If individuals prepare well, they can enter the world smoothly. In this stage, even though no one can assume the future of their life, youth are absorbed in unjustified optimism, underestimation of difficulties, exaggerated expectations, or negative attitudes. Thus adolescence is called the "unbearable age."[5]

Jung defines human psyche as growing throughout one's life phases. It is not fixed or determined. Psyche is always unfolding from the cradle to the grave.[6] At the same time, Jung insists that there is a polarity of the human psyche. In other words, he thinks that there is always a psychic tension which brings out some energy for life.[7] Through this psychic tension, Jung believes, human psyche strives to achieve a wholeness.

> But since everything living strives for wholeness, the inevitable one-sidedness of our conscious life is continually being corrected and

compensated by the universally human in us, whose goal is the ultimate integration of conscious and unconscious, or better, the assimilation of the ego to a wider personality.[8]

In this sense he rejects Freud's psychological theory which insists that childhood's influences are so crucial to determine one's stages of adulthood that life is determined by them. But Jung believes that life has a teleological goal through psyche process. So to speak, the psyche of human beings strives to reestablish and reevaluate bad influences from childhood and moves toward the telos. So Jung says that the process of life cycle moves from the ego to the self. And he calls this process individuation. But here we need to understand how the ego is related to the self in Jung's psychology. According to Jung the ego, which is rooted in the self and grows based on the self's foundation, is regarded as a subordinated part of the self. In this view, the ego is an element which knows about the self and can explain the self.[9] The ego is, by definition, subordinate to the self and is related to it like a part of the whole to which the ego is neither opposed nor subjected, but merely attached and about which it revolves[10] In other words, as body is important to soul the ego is important to the self. This is why we need to reconcile between the ego and the self, not destroy the ego for the self. Jung believes that the encounter of the self and the ego brings about the experience of rebirth.[11] This process, encountering the self, is also called "coming to selfhood," "individuation," or "self-realization,"[12] because it is a creative integration between the unconscious and consciousness, through which ego-centered personality experiences a universal encounter with the self through reorientation.[13] Jung also points out that this concern for " coming to selfhood, " or "self-realization" is a given destiny. It is a vocation whose aim is wholeness and integration of personality.

> True personality is always a vocation and puts its trust in it as in God, despite its being, as the ordinary man would say, only a personal feeling. But vocation acts like a law of God from which there is no escape. The fact that many a man who goes his own way ends in ruin means nothing to one who has a vocation. He must obey his own law, as if it were a demon whispering to him of new and wonderful paths. Anyone with a vocation hears the voice of the inner man: he is called.[14]

As it is well described in the event of incarnation, those who are in the individuation process experience a transformation called the "journey toward wholeness". But as there was suffering in incarnation, sufferings are expected in this journey.

The characteristics of "coming to selfhood" can be divided into three categories: First, the human psyche's natural tendency toward wholeness; Secondly, the reconciling tendency toward a goal, self-actualization; Lastly, the tendency to seek the meaning of life. Summarizing these categories, we can say that psychologically speaking, individuation is the reconciliation process between the unconscious and consciousness.[15] And religiously speaking, it is a religious desire for rebirth. In other words, religious maturity and rebirth equal psychological maturity and wholeness. Psychological reconciliation of unconscious and consciousness is the rebirth of religious desire. The striving toward wholeness and integration is a universal phenomena, so humanity's lopsided conscious life is challenged to be corrected and reconciled by the archetypal unconscious. But this kind of tendency does not happen intensively until midlife. The universal tendency to achieve wholeness and integration is a religious quest. In this process the self is considered as the pattern of the image of God and of individuation

With these concepts of life Jung compares the life cycle to the sun's cycle, and so divides the life cycle into two main periods: the morning and the afternoon. These main periods are divided into four categories: childhood, early maturity, middle age, and late maturity.[16] In talking about the stages of life what concerned Jung was the middle age. So he was the first psychologist to analyze the phenomenon of the mid-life crisis. Because of this he has been called the father of adult developmental psychology.[17]

Personal Unconscious and Collective Unconscious

Jung's understanding of the personal unconscious and the collective unconscious is another crucial element of understanding mid-life crisis, because the meaning of the collective unconscious is crucial to an explanation of mid-life crisis. For this section I researched Jung's understanding of the collective unconscious and compared it to Freud's understanding of the personal unconscious. This comparative study can highlight us Jung's unique understanding of mid-life crisis, because he believes that mid-life crisis is rooted in the psyche movement of the collective unconscious. Freud was once Jung's best friend and respected teacher, and Jung was regarded as the successor of Freud. Jung was very impressed after reading Freud's *The Interpretation of Dreams* in 1903, because the book implied the potentiality of explaining regarding the mechanism of repression, which Jung had studied in his *word association* experiments. They first met in Vienna in March of 1907 and talked thirteen hours without stopping. Jung's first impression of Freud was of a great teacher who was very intelligent.[18] But their friendship, which continued for twelve years, broke down and they became opponents. Though Jung and Freud were friends for twelve years, why did Jung break away from Freud? The split was based on Jung's different perspectives on the collective unconscious and the personal unconscious.

In order to speak of the cause of the break up with Freud, I want to first discuss Freud's biomedical model, because with it we can understand more succinctly Jung's psychological theory regarding mid-life. Fundamentally, they had different perspectives and understandings of the human unconscious. Freud borrowed the principles of biology and physics to explain the function of the mind. He regarded the mind as a mechanical apparatus that processed forces which were in a container in which they moved like a fluid. When energy was blocked it would build pressure. In this sense Freud used Darwin's biological postulates to explain human beings' two instincts, the sexual instinct and the aggressive instinct, which preserve the human self.[19] And he remarked that the two instincts are the seed of conflict. Why do these instincts bring out conflict? In his famous illustrative story, the Oedipus Complex, Freud insisted that boys have anxiety about castration by the father, and girls, who have experienced themselves as already castrated, feel the fear of abandonment by her mother. Thus, one's awareness of these instincts creates an intense anxiety in the personal unconscious, because such impulses are socially forbidden. He believed that this conflict and anxiety continued throughout one's life. It is called repression in the personal unconscious. In this perspective, Freud believed that sexual repression is deeply associated with the personal unconscious. Based on this fact, he argued that "sexual activity or sexual individuality" can provide a very significant meaning for analysis.[20] Thus we can conclude Freud's theory as follows: First, Freud's classic psychoanalytic theory is deterministic. All human behavior is determined by the personal unconscious over which individuals have no power of control. In Freud, determinism continues through all the stages of one's life, subsequently dominating personality and behavior. Secondly, according to Freud conflict always remains in one's life. Humans are animals of conflict, conflict not only between individuals and society, but also within one's self. Thirdly, personal unconscious plays a crucial role in determining one's behaviors, but it cannot be known to people. So even intentional efforts to change one's personality traits are ineffective. Lastly, according to Freud, dream interpretation is the only way to know about the human unconscious which determines one's behaviors. Thus, dream interpretation provides vital clues to interpret the unconscious determining one's behaviors.[21] In these ways, Freud's viewpoints on humanity are pessimistic.

Whereas Freud believes that personal unconscious determines one's life, Jung sees a larger unconscious which encompasses the personal unconscious. He believes that life is not only determined by past experiences but also influenced by one's willingness to create the future. Conflicts, coming from one's personal unconscious, are important to understanding human beings, but one's teleological goal also influences one's life. Jung points out the fault of Freud's psychology as follow:

> In Freud's view, as most people know, the contents of the unconscious are reducible to infantile tendencies which are repressed because of their incompatible character. Repression is a process that begins in early childhood under the moral influence of the environment and continues throughout life.....Although from one point of view the infantile tendencies of the unconscious are the most conspicuous, it would nonetheless be a mistake to define or evaluate the unconscious entirely in these terms.[22]

Of course, Jung accepts some parts of Freud's theory, such as sexual interest bringing out psychic conflicts in children, but Jung thinks that even children try to resolve this conflict in their early stages rather than be absorbed in it.[23] Jung could not accept Freud's definition of the personal unconscious. It became the most debatable issue to Jung. Furthermore what Jung believes is that the Oedipus and Electra complexes in Freud's theory, desiring to attach to the opposite sex of parent and wishing to get rid of the same sex of parent, are a yearning to return to become the prototype oneness with the mother.[24] In this perspective even though Jung accepted some part of the theory of the personal unconscious, he indicated the limitation of it.[25] Jung could not accept the tendency to render all causes of life to the personal unconscious, which does not allow for the existence of the collective unconscious that encircles the personal unconscious.[26] Jung clearly indicates the difference between the personal unconscious and the collective unconscious, and how much the influence of collective unconscious is crucial to people.

> ...this personal unconscious rests upon a deeper layer, which does not

derive from personal experience and is not a personal acquisition but is inborn. This deeper layer I call the *collective unconscious*. I have chosen the term "collective" because this part of the unconscious is not individual but universal; in contrast to the personal psyche, it has contents and modes of behaviors that are more or less the same everywhere and in all individuals. It is, in other words, identical in all men and thus constitutes a common psychic substrate of a suprapersonal nature which is present in every one of us.[27]

What Jung emphasizes is that the personal unconscious is important to one's life but there is a collective unconscious which is more influential to human behaviors than the personal unconscious. Thus Jung explains his unique theory of the "collective unconscious." He emphasizes that the collective unconscious is the crucial key that affects one's psyche function unconsciously. Jung believes that the collective unconscious is a reservoir which can contain archetypes. In this collective unconscious we have experienced archetypes throughout human history. Jung believes that archetypes are the common experience inherited through the history of humankind. He mentioned the following when he had an interview with Richard Evans. The content of the interview shows how much humans have been influenced absolutely but unconsciously by the collective unconscious.

Well, you know what a behavior pattern is the way in which a weaver bird builds its nest. That is an inherited form in him...And so man has, of course, an inherited scheme of functioning. You see, his liver, his heart, all his organs, and his brain will always function in a certain way, following its pattern...It is quite certain, however, that man is born with a certain functioning, a certain way of functioning, a certain pattern of behavior which is expressed in the form of archetypal image or archetypal forms...The archetypes are, at the same time, dynamic. They are instinctual images that are not intellectually invented.[28]

Jung also notes:

The contents of the collective unconscious are the results of the psyche functioning of our whole ancestry; in their totality, they compose a natural world-image, the condensation of millions of years of human experience....All mythology and all revelations come from this matrix of experience, and all our future ideas about the world and man will come from it likewise.[29]

The personal unconscious includes all psychic contents, which have been forgotten during the stages of the individual's life. This means that the personal unconscious is composed of psyche complexes which do not appear on the surface consciousness because it is repressed. But the collective unconscious is not individually acquired. It is inherited through tradition and mitigation.

> The collective unconscious is a part of the psyche which can be negatively distinguished from a personal unconscious by the fact that it does not, like the latter, owe its existence to personal experience and consequently is not a personal acquisition. While the personal unconscious is made up essentially of contents which have at one time been conscious but which have disappeared from consciousness through having been forgotten or repressed, the contents of the collective unconscious have never been in consciousness, and therefore have never been individually acquired, but owe their existence exclusively to heredity. Whereas the personal unconscious consists for the most part of complexes, the contents of the collective unconscious is made up essentially of archetypes.[30]

What Jung wants to point out is that the collective unconscious is not inherited from personal things, but from the collective experiences, which are considered irresistible. In a word, the collective unconscious is more than human instincts. Jung argues that as individuals are not separated from family and society, the human unconscious needs to be understood in terms of the social unconscious which means the collective unconscious. Just as there is society outside of individuals there is a collective unconscious outside of the personal unconscious. Thus, the collective unconscious affects personal consciousness and unconsciousness.[31] There are numerous tribes, families, and nations that have existed through human history. Their experiences are various, depending on their living situations. But, nevertheless there are archetypal experiences which transcend the variety of human situations. Jung suggests that proof for the existence of the collective unconscious is as follows. First of all, he thinks that a human being is not merely a separated being, which has its own uniqueness, but a collective one. The term "Human being" itself proves that we are the same beings. Secondly, the reason that we are collective beings can be proved in terms of the structure of human brains. The structure of the brain brings out different characteristics of individuals but, simultaneously, its mental functions make possible collective and universal functions to humankind.[32]

Male mid-life crisis/identity implies that there is a collective unconscious which causes most male mid-lifers to experience mid-life crisis. Because of this general experience, in Jung's perspective, it is not appropriate to analyze the experience based on the personal unconscious and experience. We need to understand the hidden meaning of the collective unconscious as we experience the crisis. Personal experiences of male mid-life crisis may demonstrate some deterministic despair and hopelessness. But as Jung indicates that the teleological viewpoint of life is more influential than the determinism of the personal unconscious; we need the inclusive understanding in the perspective of the collective unconscious regarding male mid-life crisis.

Mid-life: Confrontation with the Unconscious

Jung thinks that life is a process which progresses from the ego to the self. But the essential movement of psyche for the searching of one's wholeness is supposed to start at mid-life.[33] Jung believes that the most influential tendency in the first half of life, the morning, is to live under the biological and social abilities, but, in the second half of life - the afternoon, the beginning of mid-life - should be lived with the different principles, because the rules of the first half of life do not fit anymore to the second of half of life. Why do the laws of morning not fit the mid-life? The reason is that the rules of the morning demand the development of a one-sided approach in highly specific directions, such as achievements, social fame, etc. This approach can result in a serious diminution of personality with lots of self-potentiality falling into the unconscious. As adolescents have difficult times and suffering when they try to adapt the rules of childhood to the adult world, those who try to apply the patterns of the first half of life to the second half of life will have damage in their souls.[34] Questions occurring in the first half of life are related to the process of narrowing identity for one's life. So the major task in the process of identity in the first stage of life is how to cope with society. But in mid-life people are forced to be involved in a wider identity. Thus, mid-lifers need to live based on the meaning of life rather than seeking self-absorptive things.[35]

> In the morning it (the sun) rises from the nocturnal sea of consciousness and looks upon the wide bright world... At the stroke of noon the descent begins. And the descent means the reversal of all the ideals and values that were cherished in the morning.[36]

In the above paragraph Jung describes the psyche stream which comes out from the inner side of humanity in the second half of life, which is called the natural psyche tendency in the afternoon of one's life cycle. Jung describes the path of mid-life in detail, comparing the first half of life and the second half of life, as follows:

> The noon of life is the moment of greatest deployment, when a man is devoted entirely to his work, with all his ability and all his will. But it is also the moment when the twilight is born: the second half of life is beginning... At midday the descent begins, determining a reversal of all the values and all the ideals of the morning.[37]

How could Jung prove that there is a different psyche stream in the second half of life? Through his continual psychotherapy counseling with patients Jung found that men usually began exhibiting neurotic problems at around forty, while women started earlier than men. Based on his experience he realized that most of his mid-life patients suffered similar kinds of psychological sufferings around age forty.[38]

> Statistics show a rise in the frequency of mental depressions in men about forty. In women the neurotic difficulties generally begin somewhat earlier. We see that in this phase of life - between thirty-five and forty - an important change in the human psyche is in preparation. At first it is not a conscious and striking change; it is rather a matter of indirect signs of a change which seems to take its rise in the unconscious.[39]

In his observations and psychotherapy Jung found that fundamental changes happened as people approached the second half of life around age forty. And as he mentions in the above paragraph, Jung regards this phenomenon as a sign of the mid-life crisis. Based on this result Jung's concern about psychological development caused him to concentrate on adult development.[40]

> Among all my patients in the second half of life-that is to say, over thirty-five, there has not been one whose problem in the last resort was not that of finding a religious outlook on life. None of them has been really healed who did not regain his religious outlook. This of course has nothing whatever to do with a particular creed or membership of a church.[41]

The above paragraph also explains what Jung experienced through his patients. What he realized from the experience was that the sufferings of patients were deeply related to religious ontological questions. All these questions are connected with metaphysical, religious and spiritual categories. These ontological questions cannot be answered through intellectual processes. Jung points out the weakness of the intellectual process, because it cannot give satisfaction to people.[42]

Jung concludes that the cause of mid-life crisis is the collective unconscious. These causes of mid-life crisis, at first, appear indirectly from one's unconscious. They appear like a slow change of one's character.[43] People begin to think of fundamental questions about life in this stage. But the answer to questions cannot be given from outer circumstances.[44] So if mid-lifers do not find out the meaning of their lives, it brings out some neurotic problems. Based on this observation, Jung believed that the neurotic problems imply one's desire to find out the answer of life through religious insights.[45] So what he realized from experiencing mid-life crisis was that the sufferings of patients were deeply related to religious ontological questions: Who am I? Where am I from? Is there eternal life after death? What is God? What have I done in past years? What does it mean to me? If it does not mean anything to me, what reason have I to live now? And Jung affirms that all these questions cannot be answered through intellectual processes.[46] So the question regarding mid-life is a kind of theological reflection in the life-process.[47] And then why do questions that occur in mid-life relate to the religious realm? Jung explains that the reason human beings have asked this kind of question in mid-life is that these are the irresistible religious questions in the human psyche, which have been inherited by people through the collective unconscious.[48] In other words, the reason for experiencing the psyche stream in mid-life is a "confrontation with the unconscious," and Jung regards this encounter as an intense emotional turning point.[49] But those who are absorbed in self-centered tendencies in the second half of life repeat the same life patterns of the first half of life. It is a tragedy in the second half of life. Those who are obsessed with the material are not willing to converse with the unconscious, because it forces the self to be confused with the material. This tendency to be involved in matter pushes people towards ego-centralism, which makes them suffer. Thus, modern people are stuck in an illness which is called "aimlessness" or "meaninglessness."

> One of the symptoms of alienation in the modern age is the widespread sense of meaninglessness. Many patients seek

psychotherapy not for any clearly defined disorder but because they feel that life has no meaning. The thoughtful psychotherapist can scarcely avoid the impression that these people are experiencing the disrupting effects not only of an unsatisfactory childhood experience, but also of an upheaval occasioned by a major cultural transition.[50]

Thus the risk as we approach mid-life is that the nearer we get to the mid-life stage, the more we have acquired benefits from our first half of life. The benefits are seen as if we discovered and achieved the right ideals and the right course. For this reason we are inclined to keep to this path even though the result is the diminution of our personality.[51] Regarding this problem, Jung points out that if we are not transformed in the second half of life, we are going to have a meaninglessness sense of longevity in modern society. It is a challenge to modern people.

...many old people prefer to be hypochondriacs, niggards, pendants, applauders of the past or else eternal adolescents-all lamentable consequences of the delusion that the second half of life must be governed by the principles of the first.[52]

Moreover we are more oriented to the ego-based tendency than to the spiritual side. Thus the task given to us is how to overcome such a tendency so that we do not lose the balance of spirituality. If thinking rationally is the only reason to exist, existence does not have any meaning. And when rationality conquers the human soul, its result is harmful.[53] In criticizing modernity's prevalent tendency to prefer the rational, Jung argues the importance of equilibrium of psyche.

What Jung worries about seriously at this point is that if people do not discover the real meaning of life during the second half of life, all benefits from contemporary culture are meaningless in spite of the fact that modern people have benefitted from advanced technology and culture. This points out the valuelessness and meaninglessness of longevity as long as we live as eternal adolescents without considering the meaning of the second half of life. It means that our appearances show that we are adults but our inner psyche is filled with the attributes of the first half of life.

Jung points out another element which interrupts our experience of the archetypal image of God. It is so-called "science" which is the culmination of human rationality. This structural influence in modern culture causes people to be stagnated, which means people are caught in a pitfall and cannot move anymore; this finally results in a lethal end because it does not allow people to think of or experience spiritual realms which exist beyond rational understanding.[54] Indeed, Jung believes that the preference toward rationalism alienates modern people from the true meaning of life.

> Anyone who cherishes a rationalistic opinion on this score has isolated himself psychologically and stands opposed to his own basic human nature.[55]

Peter Homans, in his book *Jung in Context*, explains the meaninglessness of life which is caused by losing the meaning of God as culture shifts to become more narcissistic. In his viewpoint this narcissistic culture is the most critical problem in contemporary society. He suggests two causes which have formed modern narcissism. First, the so-called "me generation" which is so ego-centered that it is seldom concerned about others. Secondly, the "me generation" has formed narcissism. Based on this theory he points out some peculiarities of narcissism such as self-seeking, inner emptiness, no values for idealizing, and grandiosity with self. Furthermore he thinks that narcissism brings negative moral consequences.[56] Peter Homans' analysis regarding modern culture tells us how much ego-centered tendency is vulnerable and destructive to humanity.[57]

> In spite of the fact that by far the larger part of mankind does not know why the body needs salt, everyone demands it none the less because of an instinctive need. It is the same in the things of the psyche. A large majority of people have from time immemorial felt the need of believing in a continuousness of life. The demands of therapy, therefore, do not lead us into any bypaths, but down the middle of the roadway trodden by humankind. And therefore we are thinking correctly with respect to the meaning of life.[58]

There is an intimate connection with human identity and human psyche just as the body needs salt. But Jung indicates a more delicate explanation regarding the meaning of life. What does it mean that "... we are thinking correctly with respect to the meaning of life, even though we do not understand what we think."? So to speak, Jung indicates that there is an irresistible stream of psyche in humans. In other words, the reason we think of the meaning of life, especially at midlife, is that there is a primordial image which causes religious thinking about human identity and meaning. The primordial image means that in human psyche there is a seed which is called the image of God. This belief is based on Jung's theory of archetypes, which emphasizes that humanity's sense of God resides eternally within the human psyche.[59] Because of this primordial image we think more deeply, thoughtfully, religiously and philosophically regarding the identity of life in the phase of mid-life.

> Do we ever understand what we think? We only understand that thinking which is a mere equation, and from which nothing comes out but what we have put in. That is the working of the intellect. But beyond that there is a thinking in primordial images-in symbols which are older than historical man; which have been ingrained in him from earliest times, and, eternally living, outlasting all generations, still make up the groundwork of the human psyche.[60]

What we have to be concerned about from the above paragraph is that human beings can find the true meaning of life when they are in harmony with the primordial image. In other words, the reason why mid-lifers are supposed to live in harmony with the primordial image is that the primordial image is an instinct. In this sense, the dilemmas of mid-life are not about occupation, but about a vocation through which we may respond to the primordial image/the image of God and by which we may experience the meaning of life.

The Self as The Archetypal Image of God

Life is regarded as a process of realizing the self from the ego in Jung's psychology. And this process is called *self-realization, coming to selfhood,* or *individuation*. In this sense, it is a process to seek the true meaning of life. And this process happens intensely in adult development.[61] In this process, what an individual can do is to have a dialogue with the unconscious in order to be no longer focused only on the ego. By this process the socially defined ego gradually gives way to a wider range of potentials that constitute the true core of selfhood. In other words, mid-life crisis/identity is a stage in which we may have a chance to experience the self/the archetypal image of God. In this way Jung emphasizes the existence of the self, and he criticizes those who insist only on the existence of the ego.[62] From this perspective he believes that this process at mid-life means the renewal of a priori archetype which is unknown to people.

> The totality images which the unconscious produces in the course of an individuation process are similar "reformation"of a priori archetype. As I have already emphasized, the spontaneous symbols

> of the self, or wholeness, cannot in practice be distinguished from a God-image...the renewal of the mind is not meant as an actual altercation of consciousness, but rather as the restoration of an original condition, an apocatastasis. This is in exact agreement with the empirical findings of psychology, that there is an ever-present archetype of wholeness...[63]

What we can see from the paragraph is that Jung does not distinguish God-image and the priori archetype and the self. All these terms have the same meaning. He considers that the final goal of human life is to recover the archetypal image of God. Thus, seeking the self, which we may experience intensively in mid-life, does not mean to produce and create that which has not existed in the human psyche, but is a renewal of the original condition which implies "an ever-present archetype of wholeness" or "the original stage of oneness with the God-image in a religious perspective."[64] It is the goal of life and the way one becomes truly oneself. The final image of governing the self is the God-image in the psyche.[65]

> Strictly speaking, the God-image does not coincide with the unconscious as such, but with a special content of it, namely the archetype of the self. It is the archetype from which we can no longer distinguish the God-image empirically...[66]

Also Jung mentions that the psyche's instinct in seeking the meaning of life in mid-life should be understood as the will of God. This is not an arbitrary will, but an absolute will which people have to learn how to handle correctly. "Seeking the meaning of life" is regarded as fate and providence, a determining power acting on people.[67] In other words, the recovering and encountering with the self in mid-life is a vocation. What Jung found through his middle-aged-patients, who visited him because of neurosis, was that most patients' problems were associated with "seeking the meaning of life." In other words, the loss of the self manifests as neurosis whose purpose is to instinctively renew the hidden, oppressed, and forgotten image of God.[68] Because of the archetypal image of God in collective unconscious, Jung thinks that "seeking the meaning of life" in mid-life is an instinctual drive like sex and hunger. The basic reason for neurosis is an instinctive response to this seeking of equilibrium. Neurosis is a psychological symptom which occurs during the struggle for equilibrium between the consciousness and the unconscious. If people do not have equilibrium between the ego and the self, they will experience a loss of vitality, flexibility and creativity. Thus Jung concluded that his mid-life patients could not experience the archetypal image of God through their daily lives, so that neurosis phenomena occurred to them. If this is so, in this phase of mid-life, we need to understand systematically what is the definition of the archetypal image of God in Jung's analytical psychology. In describing the etymological origin of archetype Jung cited St. Augustine's definition in order to explain the image of God as a primordial image. According to Jung, the term of archetype was used in the time of St. Augustine and it had the same meaning as "idea" in the Platonic usage. In the third century, God was described as the "archetypal light," which implies that God is the origin of all light and 'pre-existent and superordinate to the phenomenon "light."'[69]

> The term "archetype" occurs as early as Philo Judaeus, with the reference of the *Imago Dei*(God-image) in man. It can also be found in Irenaeus, who says: "The creator of the world did not fashion these things directly from himself but copied them from archetypes outside himself.....because it tells us that so far as the collective unconscious contents are concerned we are dealing with archaic or-I would say-primordial types, that is, with universal images that have existed since the remotest times.[70]

But the meaning of archetype, the archetypal image of God, does not merely mean some idea inherited from the premodern world. It is more than the idea. Jung prefers to call it "an inherited mode of psychic functioning" rather than an idea.[71] This is not a vague idea, but the reality of the psyche. In other words, "the image of God" which is regarded as a universal image in humans does not mean "thought," "concept," or "idea," but the reality of psychic function which occurs intensively in mid-life.

> This term (archetype) is not meant to denote an inherited idea, but rather an inherited mode of psychic functioning, corresponding to the inborn way in which the chick emerges from the egg, the bird builds its nest, a certain kind of wasp stings the motor ganglion of the caterpillar, and eels find their way to the Bermuda. In other words, it is a "pattern of behavior." This aspect of the archetype, the purely biological one, is the proper concern of scientific psychology.[72]

In mentioning the origin of archetypes Jung regards it as "pattern of behavior," which means that it is imprinted on the human psyche as a blueprint. Based on this perspective the archetype is called the "impersonal" or "transpersonal unconscious."[73] The reason it affects all human life is that its influence is absolute to human beings. The evidence regarding this assertion is that motivating the human unconscious by archetype has inspired some mystical ideas regarding it throughout human history including now. "The image of God" is the function of psyche as a pattern of human behavior, which is deeply rooted in the collective unconscious. Because of this powerful influence, the role of archetype is considered as fate and destiny to humanity. Fate or destiny means that we cannot resist the influence of it.[74] Comparing the meaning of the archetype with the meaning of fate and destiny, Jung emphasizes that archetype exists continually even though human consciousness denies it repeatedly. Thus, this unchangeable and permanent archetype has influenced all ages and past and present, and will affect the future.[75] How can it affect even future generations? Jung insists that the inherited archetypes are not experiences, but forms without contents. As we encounter some situations, these motivate the inherited archetypes. And in this context we actively thirst for the contents of the archetype.

> There are as many archetypes as there are typical situations in life. Endless repetition has engraved these experiences into our psyche constitution, not in the form of images filled with content, but at first only as *forms without content*, representing merely the possibility of a certain type of perception and action. When a situation occurs which corresponds to a given archetype, that archetype becomes activated and a compulsiveness appears, which, like an instinctual drive, gains its way against all reason and will, or else produces a conflict of pathological dimensions...[76]

What we can see from the above is that the archetypes, the unconscious images of the instinct, are prototypes of instinctual behavior. Jung hints that archetypes themselves may penetrate and offer some clues to "the very ground of the universe."[77] In this perspective, Jung believes that even though tradition is going to be destroyed, human's nostalgia for God should occur again because human beings, in their psyche, have the most fundamental structure to understand God.[78] The human tendency and desire to seek the meaning of life in terms of seeking the image of God is stronger than passion and love. It is humanity's' thirsty desire.

> The longing for a god (might) be a passion welling up from our darkest, instinctual nature, a passion unswayed by any outside influences, deeper and stronger perhaps than the love for a human person.[79]

Humanity, since its creation, has been looking for God who is the fundamental ground of human beings. As an infant seeks its mother, seeking the archetypal image of God is an instinct. It is a nostalgia for the ground and the source from which we are originated.[80] As a wanderer wants to return home, human beings seek the lost archetype so that they may identify themselves.

The reason why male mid-lifers suffer from mental depression is that we are negligent to the archetypal image of God in the collective unconscious: The reason for suffering can be divided into two categories. First is humanity's instinct which has been inherited through the collective unconscious. Second are personal experiences which make mid-lifers remote from the archetypal image of God. Talking about the mid-life crisis, Jung insists that the typical stream of psyche happens in mid-life. Because of this he believes that people have neurotic experiences. So what Jung wants for his patients who are in this mid-life time and reveal some neurosis phenomena is that they approach the self rather than be treated for neuroses, because he believes that the meaninglessness of humans is deeply connected to religious things, and the neuroses are due to the loss of a spiritual center.[81] Thus Jung thought that the confrontation with "the self" in the human psyche had a transformative power, because experiencing the self means to encounter the origin of origins. Jung mentions how much one's religious outlook is important to heal the crisis of midlife, because he believes that true faith is related to the archetypal structure of the psyche.[82] According to Harley Chapman, who studied three methodological approaches to Jung's science, it is important to realize that religious experiences are deeply related to the process of psychological transformation. He believes that, to Jung, religious experiences simply are the experience of the existence of an archetypal image of God within the human psyche.[83] The archetypal image of God carries a psychic energy and this energy is regarded as the numinous experience in Jung's psychology. The numinous implicates an abundance of meaning, such as the formation of our mental make-up, power, emotional power, autonomy, and the archetypal image of healing power. In this perspective the numinous experience, encountering the self, becomes Jung's main concern for helping the mid-lifers. But how can people experience the self? Jung found that there is a correlation between the active encounter with the unconscious and the self. As it were, in order to be transformed people need a conscious correlation of the ego with the unconscious.[84]

> As a result of the integration of conscious and unconscious, his ego enters the "divine realm, where it participates in "God's suffering."

> The cause of the suffering is in both cases the same, namely "incarnation," which on the human level appears as "individuation."[85]

The encounter with the self is an encounter with something beyond ordinary reality. It has a numinous quality, and carries a spiritual infusion of energy. Thus, we may say that, in terms of religious words, "the self" is the issue of rebirth and renewal in a personal life. As we reflect on Jung's concept of the numinous, it clarifies more internal psyche phenomena which are hidden in the collective unconscious. But Jung emphasizes not only the spirit in human psyche but also the Spirit. He writes

> It is a misunderstanding to accuse me of having made out of this an 'immanent God' or a 'God-substitute.' This 'self' never at any time takes the place of God, though it may perhaps be a vessel for divine grace.[86]

What we conclude from this paragraph is that Jung does not identify the self with God, but thinks that the self is the place for divine grace. Jung obviously distinguished the difference between the self and God. He recognizes not only the self in human psyche, but also accepts that there is God is beyond human beings. What Jung wants to emphasize through the above paragraph is that the image of God is in the human psyche, and we cannot expect the encounter with God if we do not recover the archetypal image of God. In other words, even though Jung compares the self to the image of God, he does not compare the self to the actuality of God. Thus Jung's concept of the self implies two different functions: the self as immanent God and the self as transcendent God.[87]

> Intellectually the self is no more than a psychological concept, a construct that serves to express an unknowable essence which we cannot grasp as such, since by definition it transcends our powers of comprehension. It might equally well, he tells us, be called the 'God within us.' The beginnings of our whole psychic life seem to be inextricably rooted in this point, and all our highest and ultimate purposes seem to be striving towards it.[88]

Here is another perspective on the self. Jung considers the self also to be a transcendent concept. He thinks that the self is beyond the personal sphere and it takes place as a religious mythologem.

> ...it [the Self] encompasses both the experienceable and the inexperienceable(or the not yet experienced)... In so far as psychic

unconscious contents is a postulate, it is a transcendental concept, for it presupposes the existence of unconscious factors on empirical grounds and thus characterizes an entity that can be described only in part but, for that part, remains at present unknowable and illimitable.[89]

In this perspective the Self is the image of the immanent God and the transcendent God. As a coin has two sides, the immanent God and the transcendent God are both images of the Self. It is an inseparable oneness.

What is the result of encountering the archetypal image of God? In order to fully understand it we need to understand it as a separate concept from individualism. Individualism means to care more about oneself than others, and is concerned with individual things not collective things. It is self-centered. Jung indicates that such individuals have destroyed collective human things. He believes that human beings are created as a collective not as individuals. So, if people pursue and seek selfish things, it demolishes human nature. And it results in the alienation of the self. Those who are stuck in individualism have an illusion that they are in the process of self-realization but, in actuality, they are in self-alienation.

> Individualism means deliberately stressing and giving prominence to some supposed peculiarity rather than to collective considerations and obligations. But individuation means precisely the better and more complete fulfillment of the collective qualities of the human being.....Now in so far as the human individual, as a living unit, is composed of purely universal factors, he is wholly collective and therefore in no sense opposed to collectivity. Hence the individualistic emphasis on one's own peculiarity is a contradiction of the basic fact of the living being. Individuation, on the other hand, aims at a living co-operation of all factors.[90]

Individualism brings out isolation in persons, family, and society, whereas encountering the archetypal image of God in mid-life forces us to realize collective qualities. In other words, moving to the center of self, the archetypal image of God, makes people live cooperatively among other people.[91] So the result of seeking the archetypal image of God is a co-operative living of all elements. And people who are in this process, compared with those who are not concerned about this process, are more faithful, trustful and sincere in their social performance.[92] People who are in this process have more concern for others. They do not withdraw themselves from others, but are concerned for and care for others, because these are the tendencies and phenomena which appear after experiencing the archetypal image of God. Although individuation is a function of the psyche, the result of it is shown in the practical contexts of human living. The movement of the archetypal image of God in mid-life implies self-realization, but the fundamental purpose of the movement in mid-life is to break one's capsulized egoistic perspectives and open toward the Spirit and altruism for common virtues. This is the deep desire for the archetypal image of God in human beings.

> This widened consciousness is no longer that touchy, egotistical bundle of personal wishes, fears, hopes, and ambitions which always have to be compensated or corrected by unconscious counter tendencies; bringing the individual into absolute, binding, and indissoluble communion with the world at large.[93]

But, simultaneously, Jung points out that we have to consider the encountering of the archetypal image of God at mid-life as a process rather a stage, because it cannot be completed in one's life. And individuals' willingness to challenge the dominant culture and "irrational ones own law" are important elements for a successful process.[94]

In conclusion, Jung believes that the procedure of human development, moving from the ego to the self, is to encounter the archetypal image of God. The archetypal image of God, which he regards as the self, resides in the collective unconscious. As the characteristics of the collective unconscious show their universality, their major content, the archetypal image of God, appears in the stage of mid-life, because it is more than human instincts. Thus the major reason that male mid-lifers experience a crisis is their nostalgia for the archetypal image of God and the present gap of experiencing it because of individual situations. In this sense the healing for mid-life identity/crisis comes from the encounter with the archetypal image of God, because the encounter should not merely provide mid-lifers with the meaning of life, but rather guide them to experience the numinous experience, the healing experience. In terms of this healing experience, mid-lifers are energized to participate intensively in the process of the archetypal image of God. Regarding the results of encountering the archetypal image of God, Jung describes that healing through the archetypal image of God will be expressed as a discarding of egoistic tendencies and caring for neighbors and community, etc. Furthermore, the encounter with the archetypal image of God can make people creative and enthusiastic people.[95] In this perspective, to Jung, the most serious problem for modern people is the spiritual problem which results in the meaningless of life because of being cut off from the collective unconscious and its archetypal image of God. From this isolation contemporary people experience spiritual stagnation.[96] In this sense a given task for mid-lifers is how to find and encounter the self, which has been neglected in modernity, because encountering the archetypal image of God can influence exocentrical tendencies in mid-lifers not only to be creative, enthusiastic and inseparative, but also caring for others, community, etc..[97]

Summary

I have researched mid-life identity/crisis in the perspective of Jung's analytical psychological theories. Jung believes that the characteristics of male mid-life crisis happen around the age of forty and are totally different from the ages of ten or twenty. Males around the age of forty fall into the mid-life stage without preparation. They think that the methods of the first half of life, which is centered on egocentricity, are going to be adaptable to the second of life. However, they are not. Why do the laws of first half of life not fit the second half of life? The problem is that the rules of the morning demand the development of a one-sided approach to highly specific directions, such as achievement. Pursuing only this goal can result in a serious diminution of personality. In other words, Jung believes that mid-life crisis is due to the loss of the archetypal image of God, which causes us to fall into the meaninglessness of life. The important process in the transition of mid-life is to revalue the first half of life in the perspective of the second half of life. And truth considered as the truth in the first half needs to be peeled out of its own camouflage to be revealed as truth in terms of the second half of life.[98] Thus, mid-life crisis is a psychic movement in terms of archetype which seeks for and recovers wholeness, the image of God. Accordingly, Jung mentions that most patients who visited him in mid-life were in neurosis because of losing the self, the archetypal image of God, and sought some religious meaning for their life. In this point, Jung indicates that mid-life crisis implies a search for religious meaning.

The question of religious traits in mid-life tends to be answered as one moves along what Jung calls the path of individuation or self-actualization. The purpose of individuation is to develop from the ego into the self. Jung is confident that the self means the archetypal image of God. As we recover it, it can provide lots of meaning, because it has a transformative power. And Jung believes that mid-life crisis is an initiative stage which forces people to be liberated from an ego-centric life and move to exo-centric viewpoints such as "caring for others," and "concerning and participating in community."[99] Jung believes that this psyche tendency of mid-life is more strong than external stimuli,[100] because it cannot be erased or nullified. The archetypal image of God, which seeks wholeness, is stronger than human instincts. In this sense, the given task of male mid-lifers is to recover and renew the depressed and hidden archetypal image of God in order to find out the true values of life.

But even though seeking the archetypal image of God is an instinctual process, the result of seeking the meaning of life is different for each person. This means that the results of individuation at mid-life depends on how one copes with its process. The mid-life transition through the self provides some initiatives to get into the real meaning of life, but if people neglect these initiatives they will be stagnated. In this aspect, the initiatives of mid-life will be given to most people, but the successful process of it is up to individual effort. Acquiring values and living habits that enable the collective unconscious to begin manifesting itself through the developed personality is the essential challenge of mid-life. What we must remember is that even though the process of realization for the archetypal image of God is a path to self-actualization, few people achieve it. This process is not an achievement but a continuous process throughout life. It is a continuous process of flux and if not, it will be in stagnation. We may say that this process in mid-life is a blessing, because it initiates people in being transformed from egocentricity to exocentricity in order to find the true meaning of life.

(Notes)

1. Carl Jung, *Modern Man in Search of a Soul*, trans.W.S. Dell and Cary F. Baynes (San Diego, New York, London: A Harvest/ HBJ Book, 1933), 114. Hereafter abbreviated as *MMSS*.
2. Ibid., 98.
3. Ibid.
4. Ibid., 99.
5. Carl G. Jung, *Collect Work*, Vol. 8.(Princeton: Princeton University, 1981), 390-91. Hereafter abbreviated as *CW*.
6. Ibid., 98.
7. *CW*. Vol. 8, 200.
8. Ibid. 292.
9. *CW*. Vol. 9-2, 5.
10. Ibid.
11. *CW*. Vol.11, 341.
12. *CW*. Vol. 7, 182.
13. Ibid., 177-78.
14. *CW* . Vol.17, 175.

15. *CW*. Vol.10, 305.
16. Carl G. Jung, *MMSS*, 114.
17. Anthony Stevens, *On Jung*, (New York, London: Penguin Book, 1990), 62.
18. C. G. Jung, *Memories, Dreams, Reflections*, ed. Aniela Jaffe (New York: Vintage Books, 1961), 146-49. Hereafter abbreviated as *MDR*.
19. Allen M. Siegel, *Heinz Kohut and the Psychology of the Self* (London and New York: Routledge, 1996), 19-37.
20. Sigmund Freud, *Leonardo da Vinci and a Memory of His Childhood* (New York: Norton, 1989), 16.
21. Dan P. McAdams, *The Person: An Introduction to Personality Psychology* (Orlando: Harcourt Brace College Publishers, 1994), 656-58.
22. *CW*. Vol. 7, 127.
23. Mary Ann Mattoon, *Jungian Psychology in Perspective* (New York: The Free Press, 1981), 166.
24. Ibid., 170.
25. *CW*. Vol. 7, 128.
26. *CW*. Vol. 9-1, 47.
27. Ibid., 3-4.
28. Richard Evans, *Conversation with Carl Jung and Reactions from Ernest Jones* (New York: Van Nostrand Reinhold Company, 1964), 47-48.
29. *CW*. Vol. 8, 380.
30. *CW*. Vol.9-1, 42.
31. *CW*. Vol. 7, 145.
32. Ibid., 147-48, 275
33. *CW*. Vol. 7, 173; Daniel Levinson et al., *The Seasons of a Man's life* (New York: Ballantine Books, 1978), 196.
34. *CW*. Vol. 8, 399-400.
35. *CW*. Vol. 7, 74.
36. Carl Jung, *MMSS*, 104.
37. Robert C. Fuller, *Religions and Life Cycle* (Philadelphia: Fortress, 1988),106.
38. Carl G. Jung, *MMSS*, 104.
39. *CW*. Vol. 8, 395.
40. Daniel Levinson, op. cit., 4.
41. *CW*. Vol. 11, 334.
42. Carl G. Jung, *Word and Image*, ed. Aniela Jaffe (Princeton: Princeton University Press, 1979), 124.
43. Carl G. Jung, *MMSS,* 104.
44. *CW*. Vol. 4, 551.
45. *CW*. Vol.11, 334..
46. Carl G. Jung, *Word and Image*, 123.
47. *CW*. Vol. 11, 64.
48. *CW*. Vol. 7, 66.
49. C. G. Jung. *MDR*, 170-199.
50. Edward F. Edinger, *Ego and Archetype*(New York & Boston: Shambala, 1992), 107.
51. *CW.*, Vol. 7, 395.

52. Ibid., 399.
53. Carl Jung, *C.G. Jung Psychological Reflections*, eds. Johande Jacobe & R.F.C. Hull (New Jersey: Princeton University, 1978), 254-65.
54. *CW*. Vol. 9-2, 109.
55. *CW*. Vol. 8, 410.
56. Peter Homans, *Jung in Context: Modernity and the Making of a Psychology* (Chicago: University of Chicago, 1995), 197.
57. Ibid.
58. Carl. G. Jung, *MMSS*, 112.
59. *CW*. Vol.11, 12.
60. Ibid.,112-13.
61. *CW*. Vol. 7, 173; Daniel Levinson et al., op. cit., 196.
62. *CW*. Vol. 9-1, 275.
63. *CW*. Vol. 9-2, 40.
64. Ibid.
65. Demaris S. Wehr, *Jung & Feminism* (Boston: Beacon Press, 1987), 84.
66. *CW*. Vol. 11, 469.
67. *CW*. Vol. 9-2, 27.
68. *CW*. Vol. 17, 175.
69. *CW*. Vol.9-1, 75
70. Ibid., 4-5.
71. *CW*. Vol. 7, 138.
72. *CW*. Vol.18, 518.
73. *CW*. Vol.7, 66.
74. *CW*. Vol.9-1, 30.
75. *CW*. Vol.7, 192.
76. *CW*. Vol.9-1, 48.
77. *CW*. Vol.11, 200.
78. *CW*. Vol. 5, 30.
79. *CW*. Vol. 7, 134.
80. *CW*. Vol.9-1, 286-87; *CW*. Vol.7, 169.
81. Robert L. Moore and Daniel J. Meckel, *Jung and Christianity* (New York: Paulist Press, 1990), 6.
82. *CW*. Vol. 5, 235.
83. Harley J. Chapman, *Jung's Three Theories of Religious Experience* (Lewiston/Queenston: The Edwin Mellen Press, 1988), 76.
84. Harry A. Senn, "Jungian Shamanism," in *Journal of Psychoactive Drugs* 21:1 (1989):118.
85. *CW*. Vol. 11, 157
86. *CW*. Vol. 10, 483.
87. Mary Ann Mattoon, *Jung Psychology in Perspective* (New York & London: Free Press, 1081), 198.
88. *CW*. Vol. 7, 250.
89. *CW*. Vol. 6, 460.
90. *CW*. Vol. 7, 173-74.
91. Ibid., 173.

92. Ibid., 174.
93. Ibid., 177.
94. *CW*. Vol. 17, 176.
95. Carl Jung, *C. G. Jung Psychological Reflections*, 265.
96. *CW*. Vol. 11, 345-46.
97. Carl Jung, *C.G. Jung Psychological Reflections*, 265.
98. *CW*. Vol. 7, 75.
99. Carl G. Jung, *Jung Psychological Reflections*, 265.
100. Carl G. Jung, *CW*. Vol. 8, 397; Anthony Stevens, *On Jung* (London, England: Penguin Books, 1990), 166.

Chapter 2

Erik H. Erikson's Psycho-social Understanding about Self-Identity in Mid-life

In this part I intend to research the meaning of mid-life identity/crisis based on Erikson's psychosocial theory. The reason I choose Erik H. Erikson to study regarding mid-life is that he is the first psychologist who systemizes the developmental stages of adulthood, generativity and stagnation. In this sense Erikson's psychosocial theory is essential for studying the mid-life transition.[1] Erikson's psychosocial understanding about the human identity process can also give us a different perspective for an understanding of male mid-life crisis.

Epigenesis Structure of Human Development

Freud's psychosexual theory is so powerful that most psychological theories, such as ego psychology, object relation psychology and self psychology, have been influenced by Freud's theory. Erik Erikson's theory was also influenced by Freud's psychosexual theory; the first five stages of Erikson's psychosocial theory are similar to Freud's biological epigenetic development stages, which are the oral stage, the anal stage, the oedipal stage, the latency stage, and the genital stage.[2] In this sense, Erikson accepts that the ego is shaped by psychological and biological factors. But as I mentioned in the previous chapter, Freud's viewpoint regarding humanity is very pessimistic. All intentional efforts to change one's personality traits have been determined by one's unconsciousness. In this perspective there is no hope for humanity. But in Erikson's psychosocial perspective on the self, a critical question rises against this pessimistic viewpoint on humanity. Who is responsible for 'I' in the present time? Is it 'I,' or someone else? According to Freud, 'I' am not responsible for my behaviors, because they were determined in the past, and cannot be changed. In this perspective, Erikson criticizes the irresponsible 'I' as being the same thing. He wrote,

> If everything goes back to childhood then everything is someone's fault and trust in the power of taking responsibility for oneself is determined.

This lopsided psychological interpretation of the self in Freud's theory has been criticized also from feminist perspectives. Joan Berzoff, in her feminist perspective, *Inside Out and Outside In*, critiques Freudian theory and explains how social contexts of the time affected Freud in forming the psychosexual theory.

> [Freud was] Born in Freibern, Moravia (now a part of the Czech Republic) in 1856 to a wool merchant. Freud moved with his family to Vienna when he was 4. At the height of the Victorian era, this city was considered to be the seat of licentiousness and sexuality in Europe. There was a facade of control and repression of sexuality within a largely Catholic culture. Yet men routinely went to prostitutes and women likewise had lovers. Women in Victorian Vienna were viewed either as sexual property among working classes, or as sexless objects with carefully prescribed social roles (Lerman 1986). In either case, women rarely were expected to fulfill their potential for whole experience. Furthermore, the absence of means for birth control made the expression of sexuality in all social classes a dangerous enterprise. Freud thus grew up in a cultural context of sexual contradictions. It was within this social context that the concept of repressed sexuality, so central to Freud's thinking, emerged.[3]

I would argue that Freud's social milieus strongly helped to formulate his psychosexual theories. So it is impossible to understand human development without understanding the interaction between the personal and social milieu, because, as indicated by Erikson, these two elements are inseparable and interactive in the formation of human personality.

Carol Gilligan also criticizes Freud's theory. According to Carol

Gilligan, the origin of the psychosexual denigration of women started with Freud's psychosexual theory. When boys experienced what Freud called the Oedipus complex, Freud needed to substitute some psychological explanation for girls who were of the same age. In his hypothesis, Freud began to compare girls' complexes to the Oedipus complex. Assuming the male perspective as normative, Freud interpreted girls' psychosexual development. Consequently, girls' "penis envy" which is caused by the lack of boys' sexual organs always has been interpreted to imply the inferiority of girls. Carol Gilligan thinks that this Freudian psychosexual concept has been generalized in our society. This generalized concept about women from Freudian theory negatively impacts the social roles expected of women.[4]

In this sense, Erikson's question regarding Freud's pessimistic-determistic psychosexual theory, for the worst fails to take into consideration the social milieu, radically reconfigures a central issue; that is who is responsible for 'I'? Freud's theory always refers to past experiences. In these perspectives, developmental psychologist Dan P. McAdams describes the difference between Freud and Erikson as follows:

> In contrast to Freud, Erikson has made a theoretical commitment to the idea that personality development can only be understood in the context of the interpersonal-social-cultural-historical environment within which it occurs. While one cannot neglect the psychosexual dimensions of human development, the stages of the life cycle are more adequately seen as psychosocial in nature, the result of repeated transactions between the individual and society. Therefore, Erikson defines development in terms of particular psychosocial issues, rather than in terms of Freud's transformations of the libido. Whereas Freud suggests that personality development ends in early adolescence with attainment of genital maturity, Erikson proposes a life-span model of development, with eight psychosocial stages extending even into old age.[5]

Erikson's theory does not stay in past experiences, but emphasizes the role of 'ego' in present times. Not that Erikson dismissed Freud's work. Erikson uses some part of Freud's epigenetic principles. In other words, we can say that Erik H. Erikson's psychosocial development theory is based on Epigenesis, which means the psychological growth of humans is like the development of a fetal organ system, because Erikson believes that the human body has its own time to grow. Similarly, human psychological potentialities have their own time to grow.[6] Epigenesis is a kind of blueprint, an architecture built into each human. Based on this theory and his experience as a clinician and theoretician he assures us that *epigenesis* is an unavoidable element to understanding psychosexual and psychosocial development. He defines *epigenesis* in detail as follows:

> Eventually, however, embryology came to understand epigenetic development, the step-by-step growth of the fetal organs, even as psychoanalysis discovered the pregenital stage of sexuality....I hope that the reader will "hear" the probability that all growth and development follow analogous patterns. In the epigenetic sequence of development each organ has its time of origin....If organs misses its time of ascendance, it is not only doomed as an entity, it endangers at the same time the whole hierarchy of organs.[7]

As he describes the meaning of epigenesis he points out both that in the development of human organs the organs have appropriate time to grow and that there are some specific developments of the human identity process in the life cycle. It means that not only each organ has its own time of growth, but also formulates identity in the process. In this sense, time is a very crucial element in the growth of organs and identity. Without the healthy development of one organ one can hardly expect the growth of the next healthy organ, because all these developments are correlated to each other. Without the successful development of one's identity or crisis at each stage, one's identity at the next stage cannot be maturely developed. All of these concepts are based on his clinical experiences.

> Whenever we try to understand growth, it is well to remember the *epigenetic principle* which is derived from the growth of organisms *in utero*. Somewhat generalized, this principle stage that anything that grows has a *ground plan*, and that out of this ground plan the *parts* arise, each part having its *time* of special ascendancy, until all parts have arisen to form a functioning whole.[8]

At least what Erikson points out in the above paragraph is that human development, from the standpoint of physiology is based on a predestined ground plan. Thus all developments of the organs are correlated and interactivated. Through appropriate interactions among organs, based on proper and healthy development, we can expect a healthy identity. In applying this concept of epigenesis to the human life cycle, he divides the life cycle into eight stages. However human development is not only influenced by the epigegenetic principle but also other elements. In order to understand the human life cycle he suggests that there are three elements, *soma, psyche*, and *ethos,* cooperating for the identity formation of each stage.

> On the basis of case-historical and life-historical experience, therefore, I can only begin with the assumption that a human being's existence depends at every moment on three processes of organization that must complement each other. There is, in whatever order, the biological process of the hierarchic organization of organ systems constituting a body(*soma)*; there is the psychic process organizing individual experience by ego synthesis(psyche); and there is the communal process of the cultural organization of the interdependence of persons(*ethos*).[9]

In other words, Erikson believes that we need to understand life on three levels and he assures us that a sound and healthy psychological and physical maturity and development can happen through the cooperative interaction of these three. The first *(soma)* includes all given constitutional conditions, including libidinal dynamic and the level/condition of the body. The second *(psyche)* is the level of ego which has its own unique way of integrating experience and the ability to cope with conflict and anxiety. Last *(ethos)* is the level of family and society, which shapes an individual's developmental history. In other words, to understand a person's life we need to figure out their personal psychological history, relationships with others, and interactions between 'I' and society. Erikson calls these three elements "triple bookkeeping" in the understanding of one's life. And it is imperative to understand and analyze human development, because all these three elements are related to the cogwheeling of the life cycle.

> ...being unable to arrive at any simple sequence and casual chain with a clear location and a circumscribed beginning, only triple bookkeeping can gradually clarify the relevance and relatives of all the known data.[10]

These three elements are linked together and are inevitable elements in the formation of one's life cycle for.[11] In this way, Erikson's analysis of humanity is not fixed in the psychosexual area, but expands and includes the interaction between all bio-social milieu.

In this sense, what Erikson emphasizes is that in the understanding of a human life cycle it is necessary to analyze the person in social and biological viewpoints, because, as the term *epigenesis* implies, there is always the interaction between persons and social milieu. So Erikson uses the technical term "cogwheeling of life cycles," which indicates mutual interaction between the developing individuals through their needs and responses and society responding to individuals' needs.

> Defenseless as babies are, there are mothers at their command, families, and traditions to give a cultural continuity to systems of tending and training. All of this, however, the human infant does need in order to evolve humanly: for this environment must provide that outer wholeness and continuity which, like a second womb, permits the child to develop his separate capacities in distinct steps, and to unify them only in a series of psychosocial crises.[12]

As he accentuates the role of family and society (*ethos*) with the interaction with biological perspectives of human beings, he mentions that there should be "crisis" in the process of human development. "Crisis" is a specific and unique key concept of Erikson's psychosocial theory, because he regards "crisis" as a given task to be solved at each stage of human development.

> Each successive step of development, then, is a potential crisis because of a radical change in perspective. Crisis is used here in a developmental sense to connote not a threat of catastrophe, but a turning point, a crucial period of increased vulnerability and heightened potential, and therefore, the ontogenetic source of generational strength and maladjustment.[13]

The crisis at each stage of the human life cycle is regarded as a crucial process for healthy development, because each crisis can prepare a person for the next stage of human development and each crisis contributes to the adult personality. We need to listen to Erikson's saying that crisis is not a threat but a "turning point." In this sense he describes the psychosocial crises of each stage. In this description, Erikson explains that there are eight stages of psychosocial development, with two formulas in each stage. These formulas are the "ego quality," which shows whether people have successful resolution of that stage or not, and the "quality maintaining" which shows whether people are successful in various social circumstances and experiences.[14]

Erikson's psychosocial theory combined with the concepts of triple bookkeeping is regarded as universal in spite of the fact that Erikson thinks that the solution for each crisis at each stage may differ because of different cultural and historical situations.[15] But Erikson does not stop mentioning the importance of basic human commonality among cultures. Even though we have different cultures there are some things we all have in common as humans.

> But here, too, it is important to realize that in the sequence of his most personal experiences the healthy child, given a reasonable amount of guidance, can be trusted to obey inner laws of development, laws which create a *succession of potentialities for significant interaction* with those who tend him. While such interaction varies from culture to culture, it must remain within the *proper rate and the proper sequence* which govern the *growth of a personality* as well as that of an organism. Personality can be said to develop according to steps predetermined in the human organism's readiness to be driven toward, to be aware of, and to interact with, a widening social radius, beginning with the dim image of a mother and ending with mankind, or at any rate that segment of mankind which "counts" in the particular individual's life.[16]

In this perspective Erikson sees that human development is predestined and also that this development will grow through the interactions with the mother and social milieus. And he maintains that as humans grow there are crises in each stage. What is important to Erikson is that in spite of the fact that his theory cannot be applied to all cultures and races, his theory provides, to some extent, the proper rate which can be applied to all cultures.

Generativity at Mid-life: Self-Identity as Immortality

Erikson's psychosocial theory suggests that there are eight stages of life. Among the eight stages of life there are three different stages of adult life: young adult, adult and old age. The crisis of intimacy versus isolation is characteristic of young adulthood. The central process of solving this crisis is the establishment of mutuality with an age-mate. The positive consequences are feelings of love and reciprocity. The second crisis is generativity vs. stagnation, and last one is integrity vs.

despair. Among these stages Erikson also indicates three crucial stages of life, even though his psychosocial theory divides the life span into eight stages. First, in an infancy period, where there is mistrust vs. trust possibility. The virtue of this stage is 'hope.' Secondly, identity vs. identity confusion in adolescence; 'fidelity' is the virtue of this stage. Lastly, generativity vs. stagnation in adulthood; 'care' is the virtue of this stage.[17] In this viewpoint, the stage of middle age, which is related to generativity vs. stagnation, has been considered one of the most important life stages. In this period, individuals begin to rethink their lives in terms of "time left to live" vs. "time since birth." Among the three stages in adulthood, middle adulthood belongs to the mid-life transition, in which one reappraises what one has done with life. This is a period when individuals psychologically begin to think that the prime of life is over and that its autumn has begun. These internal psychological moods cause people to think of their past as well as their future. People may think, " How long have I lived?" " How much time do I have to live?"[18]

The two contrasting psychological phenomena for middle adulthood, generativity and stagnation, describe two possible results. Generativity means a concern partly for the psychological welfare of one's children, and partly for humanity in general.[19] Why do people who are in this stage generally think of posterity and their own destiny? In a word, their thinking represents a concern for the disappearing generation as well as the emerging, growing generations. They begin to realize human destiny/limitation and how it is valuable to live as a human being in a short term called life. Erikson defines generativity using three levels: procreativity, productivity, and creativity.

> I can only repeat that the generational cycle links life cycles together by confronting the older generation's generativity with the younger one's readiness to grow. This has three dominant aspects: the procreative one which gives birth and responds to the needs of the next generation; the productive one, which integrates work life with family life within the political and technological framework; and the creative one, which elaborates cultural potentials within the emerging world image.[20]

The three categories of generativity show the collective meaning of generativity. But he defines the inclusive concept of generativity in his book *The Life Cycle Completed* as follows:

To adulthood(our seventh stage) we have assigned the critical antithesis of *generativity* vs. *self-absorption and stagnation.* Generativity, we said, encompasses *procreativity, productivity,* and *creativity*, and thus the generation of new beings as well as of new products and new ideas, including a kind of self-generation concerned with further identity development.[21]

Erikson, in the above paragraph, describes that generativity not only includes the three concepts but also involves "self-generation" concern and identity. In other words, as mid-lifers encounter or practice the three inclusive meanings of generativity they can develop their identity. As we see in Erikson's definition of generativity, these three levels enunciate that generativity, in general meaning humanity's instinct to leave something valuable, physically and mentally, to the next generation. Erikson refers to generativity as the "instinctual power."[22] In this instinctual power, people who are in adulthood want to leave something for successive generations. There is a desire to teach something, which is creative, to the next generation. By leaving some valuable/creative things to next generation, people issue the meaning of life in generativity.[23] Thus mid-lifers attempt to outlive the self. But what is most important among the categories of the definition of generativity is the concern for guiding and establishing the next generation.[24] Thus, even though the other two categories belong to the meaning of general generativity, the essence of generativity means to have concerns for the next generation.

Generativity, then, is primarily the concern in establishing and guiding the next generation...And indeed, the concept of generativity is meant to include such more popular synonyms as *productivity* and *creativity*, which, however, cannot replace it.[25]

Erikson's work has been considered and expanded on by many psychologists, but I have chosen the following seven figures; I briefly summarize their theories. John Korte's[26] explanation supports Erikson's definition of generativity. Korte categorizes generativity into four types. First of all, all categorized generativity can be defined as follows: "a desire to invest one's substance in forms of life and work that will outlive the self."[27]

The first is biological, which encompasses fertility as demographers and birth planners speak of it: the begetting, bearing, and nursing of children... Only in biological transmission is material substance passed from the body of the progenitor to that of the creation... Distinct from biological generativity is the parental type, which is expressed in feeding, clothing, sheltering, loving, and disciplining offspring and initiating them into the family's traditions...Technical generativity, the third type, is accomplished by teachers at all stations of the journey through life, who pass on skills to those less advanced than themselves... Cultural generativity means creating, renovating , and conserving a symbol system-the "mind" of a culture-explicitly passing it on to successors.[28]

Dan P. McAdams[29] explains in terms of Erikson's psychological theory that there are two crucial elements as people approach mid-life. First is the influence of immortality at mid-life. It is about human destiny in terms of life vs. death. Death is no longer purely the concern of others at one's mid-life. Before midlife immortality is considered to be other people's concern. But, in mid-life, people feel and realize that the first half of life is gone, and the last of half of life is left. As it were, the meaning of mortality approaches during middle age.[30] Elliott Jaques'[31] study, which researched 310 male genius artists' biographical information and works, shows an intimate relationship between mid-life and death.[32] Thus, there is some intimate relationship between the fear of death and generativity in midlife. In midlife, the concept of death is no longer other people's problem. It is not a story of others anymore. It is now my story that I have to go through. This is practical in approaching middle age. Some of our parents, uncles, aunts, and even friends are passing away. This is the story that middle aged people are supposed to hear in their life journeys. The second reason is a "need to be needed." It means that as we get into the stage of mid-life, society expects mid-lifers to be successful contributors to family, community, society, etc. What society expects from mid-lifers is that they are to be a numinous model who can judge evil and transmit values to the future generations.

Bernace Neugarten mentions that middle aged people are located inbetween a passing generation as parents, and a coming generation of their children.[33] What they feel between these generations is generativity. Erikson also mentions that the inevitable end of life causes the crisis of generativity.[34] Robert Lifton also explains also well how middle age's generative tendency is related to immortality.

> [immortality as] a compelling universal urge to maintain an inner sense of continuous symbolical relationship, over time and space, with the various elements of life. [immortality will be] living on through and in one's sons and daughters and their sons and daughters. One's writing, one's teaching, one's human influences, great or humble, will live on; that one's contribution will not die.[35]

Thus, because of the concern for immortality which is accomplished through future generations, parents feel that their children fulfill their own hopes, and desire what the parents did not realize in their life span.[36] So, parents wish, desire and project values on to their children as a sort of immortality.

Ernest Becker, Pulitzer prize winner, who wrote *The Denial of Death*, insists that the human mind is connected with immortality, even though the body is associated with mortal flesh. On one side, spiritually, humans are rooted in immortality, while on the other side they are associated with mortality. But he believes that the main motivation which spurs human activities is immortality. In other words, the fear of death compels humanity to be involved in heroism in which people create and produce valuable things and cultures. Thus, in a sense, inevitable fear of death produces the concept of immortality and this desire to be immortal is expressed in leaving some philosophical or artistic learning to the next generation through generativity.[37] Becker's explanation supports Erikson's interpretation of generativity, the instinctive drive. Regarding Erikson's definition of generativity Don Browning defines generativity as follows:

> Generativity, not just libidinal sexuality, is the true archaic foundation of man. Certainly for Erikson, man is a creature of desire; but desire, for him, is more than sexual release or sensual enjoyment. Desire is complex coordination of a wide range of instinctive patterns which all aim toward self-expression and self-confirmation through generativity. Erikson speaks of a "wish" for generativity. In addition, he refers generativity as the "instinctual power behind various forms of selfless "caring." [38]

Don Browning[39] believes that, to Erikson, generativity is regarded as having a relationship between the archaic and the teleologic, because both are rooted in it. Thus generativity means most primitive and most basic. Simultaneously generativity includes the goal of existence. The goal of existence not only means to create biological care and procreation but also means to provide a total environment, including family and human world.[40] In this sense, Erikson compares generative men and religious reformers. He believes that true generative men are the true religious reformers.

> We have seen how deeply Gandhi at times minded having to become a householder, for without this becoming committed to a normal course of life by child marriage, he might well have been a monastic saint instead of what he became: politician and reformer with an honorary sainthood. For the true saints are those who transfer the state of householdership to the house of God, becoming father and mother, brother and sister, son and daughter, to all creation, rather than to their own issue.[41]

In this perspective, generativity is not limited to only one trend, such as having and raising children. There are many ways to be generative, such as community involvement, creative works, etc. But what we have to remember about the tendencies of generativity is that generativity is "the desire to invest one's substance in forms of life and work that will outlive the self". Surely these desires in mid-life imply humanity's desire for immortality through one's commitment to family, society and future generations. Thus, generativity is a human instinct which sublimes human limitations in terms of immortality and the need to be needed.

Theoretically and philosophically, the wish to be generative in middle age is the unconscious wish to live forever. But, in reality, people in middle age know that to live forever is impossible. In this situation, what they want to do is to project their values, works, and philosophy to successive generations, others and community. By doing this, even though their bodies die, their souls become immortal to upcoming generations.

Erikson indicates that the tendencies of generativity at mid-life are related to the meaning of immortality. Concern about younger generations, future generations, and ideal society are due to this immortality which we have to experience as we pass through adulthood. In this sense the three categories of generativity imply some new creations of products, ideas and new generations, because all these things show humans' common desire for immortality.

Why do people have such a generative instinct in adulthood? What is the main reason people are concerned about generativity? Erikson explains the relationship between generativity and immortality.

> The capacity for grand-generativity incorporates care for the present with concern for the future-for today's younger generations in their futures, for generations not yet born, and for the survival of the world as a whole. It contributes to the sense of immortality that becomes so important in the individual's struggle to transcend realistic despair as the end of life approaches, inevitably....concern for their children dominates both their reflection on earlier life's guidance and nurturance and their current involvement in caring. For most of the people, it seems that parenthood has been the primary focus of adulthood responsibility.[42]

Erikson explains the meaning of "the need to be needed" as follows.

> An adult must be ready to become a numinous model in the next generation's eyes and to act as a judge of evil and a transmitter of ideal values. Therefore, adults must also do ritualize being ritualizers; and there is an ancient need and custom to participate in some rituals that ceremonially sanction and reinforce that role. This whole adult element in ritualization we may simply call the generative one. It includes such auxiliary ritualizations as the parental and the didactic, the productive and the curative.[43]

In other words, there are specific expectations society has for mid-lifers, such as being mentors, didactic in terms of generativity. But we might ask a question: from where do these tendencies come? What is their origin? Regarding these questions I think that the question of immortality existed before mid-lifers had generative tendencies. Because, first of all, mid-lifers had felt immortality first and they wondered how they might live as meaningful beings.

The concept of immortality defined by Erikson implies that generativity is associated with the ultimate human desire to transcend one's finite self in terms of leaving and giving some values to future generations. But as Erikson's theory pointed out previously, each stage of human development is correlated with a previous stage of life. In this sense, to be generative men, in Erikson's perspective, we need previously good-enough stages because these stages are crucial in the formation of generativity. So it is imperative to understand generativity in terms of how the social milieu has affected to mid-lifers. Erikson argues that mature adults show generative tendencies in terms of interaction through *soma, psyche,* and *ethos.*

> All the strengths arising from earlier developments in the ascending order from infancy to young adulthood (hope and will, purpose and skill, fidelity and love) now prove, on closer study, to be essential for the generational task of cultivation strength in the next generation. For this is, indeed, the "store" of human life.[44]

Generativity as Instinctive Drive

Sometimes we may ask whether generativity is general or not, because our society expects the tendencies of generativity from mid-lifers. But can people who live in a different culture experience generativity? Can all people experience generativity? Erikson was also asked the same question. To this question, Erikson replies positively in an interview. He believes that generativity can be applied to all kinds of people; it is a general phenomenon.

> **Hall**: It's easy for me to see how a childless artist or a writer or a teacher can sublimate generativity in their work. Now how does a plumber do it?
> **Erikson**: Don't underestimate the generative contributions of a good plumber. Also, he or she may be a church member who can do something for all the children in this community. And he or she is still a voter.[45]

Generativity is not limited to special people and classes. It is a universal inner desire for immortality. In other words, Erikson defines generativity as "the instinctual power behind various forms of selfless 'caring.'"[46] Thus, it does not depend upon what we have or what we are in the social system, because it is a human instinct which cannot be erased by external milieus. In other words, it is instinctual to all humans. In this sense Dan McAdams's definition of generativity is also very inclusive.

> Generativity has been variously described as a biological drive to reproduce oneself, an instinctual need to care for and be needed by others, a philosophical urge for transcendence and symbolic immortality, a developmental sign of maturity and mental health in

adulthood, and a social demand to create a productive niche in society.[47]

What Dan McAdams suggests in the above paragraph is that generativity has two categories as I mentioned in previous pages. One is immortality, through which we can see how human beings have experienced human destiny and how this despair can be sublimated through positive attitudes toward human life. The second category is the "need to be needed," through which humans are asked to be valuable beings. In other words, broadly speaking regarding the second category, as long as humans live they need to be valuable beings who can contribute invisibly or visibly to others, and this contribution makes people feel their valuable meaning among others. In this sense, Erikson mentions that generativity is a kind of instinctual power.[48] Don Browning argues that generativity comes from the archaic human unconsciousness.[49] Don Browning explains that for Erikson generativity means "the true archaic foundation of man."[50] This archaic unconsciousness/foundation is associated with the roots of human ontological questions, including the origin and the end of the human species. Humanity has been challenged by these ontological questions regarding the meanings of humans throughout human history. It means that figuring out the origin of humanity and answering the questions about life and death have been formed in culture throughout history. Don Browning says that generativity equals the archaic and teleologic view about one's future. If we make a formula, it is like this: generativity=the archaic+the teleologic vision for life. In this sense, the archaic is deeply related to human unconsciousness which provides answers to human's ontological questions. The teleological view shows how people have maturity as the goal of their existence.[51] In order to have a right and clear goal of existence, the archaic, which can provide a true meaning of life, is the inevitable element.[52] In other words, basically, after clarifying one's identity in terms of the archaic, we may have a right goal of future existence in terms of the teleological perspective. In combining these two elements, the archaic and the teleological thrust for the future, we may have generative tendencies. If so, what is the archaic? In order to understand it, we need some religious anthropological interpretation of it. I think that Mircea Eliade can give a clear understanding of it. He believes that the origin of religions and reverence to God occur as premodern people realize their mortality. In the history of religions, to the historian of religions, the concept of the sacred is intimately connected with the idea of the meaning of being and of existence. Eliade describes the history of religions not by revealing the phenomena of religious experiences but by reminding us of the process of self-understanding in terms of the sacred.[53] Throughout the history of religions what humans want is to figure out the meaning of their identity. Thus, we may say that there is some salient relationship between the sacred and human identity.[54]

Desiring to solve human identity in terms of the sacred in the premodern world and the concern for successive generations is a continuing desire of humanity. In this sense, the sacred becomes the perspective for understanding the world and the meaning of life. So long as we exist as humanity, this question will be repeatedly asked by us and our posterity. Throughout human history, this question regarding the identity of being and concern for the next generation has remained an archetype, because generativity is a human instinct which comes from the archaic and the teleological thrust. In this sense, Don Browning states that a "generative man is a religious man,"[55] which can be associated with generativity as a human instinct. As it were, generativity implies religious meaning. The concerns of generative people as mid-lifers need to be understood in the contexts of religious meaning.

> Generative man is a religious man. His religion provides him with a commanding world image and a vigorous ritual enactment which sums up, yet somehow renews and enriches, the rituals of everyday life, both those of his children and of himself, and those of his own childhood. His religion sanctions him to indulge in a "generalized generativity of institutions." He too must become, to some extent, a "numinous model" and must learn to act as the "judge and the transmitter of traditional ideals or of innovating ideas."[56]

Erikson mentions Homo Religious, in *The Life Cycle Completed*, *Gandhi's Truth*, and *Young Man Luther*, as examples of those who have a deep religious sense. Homo Religious people are those who struggle with existential conflicts and provide meaningful relationships with the people, bringing a new converted identity for all generations; in terms of these results, they create renewed social contexts in which people are encouraged, motivated, relocated and sanctified. They always believe that there is absolute reality which transcends the world and manifests in the world and sanctifies the world.[57] Homo Religious people transcend ordinary people's concerns. In this perspective, those who are generative are called "homo religious" people (Erikson) "religious man" (Don Browning), and "creative ritualist" (Donald Capps). Humanity belongs to category of Homo Religious (Religious Humanity). Whether we know about it or not, at least we are involved in it unconsciously even in modernity.

Here is a further deep explanation of generativity. Eugene J. Wright, in his book *Erikson, Identity and Religion*, argues that generativity is a signal of the dimension of ultimacy. What we know from the following paragraph is that generativity is an instinctive power, which I prefer to call "archetype," in human unconsciousness.

> To generate rather than stagnate is certainly a dimension of creativity hinting at a Creator who created in his own image. He endowed his creation to be co-workers with himself, as the Judeo-Christian tradition has long taught. Generativity, with care as its virtue, signals of dimension of ultimacy beyond the ordinary...[58]

Donald Capps compares generativity to the spirit of empathy. He suggests that caring concern in generativity can be energized by the spirit of empathy. Through it, people realize others' demands in the perspective of a deeply caring God.[59] Thus generativity is an instinctive drive rooted in the unconscious which is regarded as a blueprint which stimulates people to be Homo Religious, through which humanity has participated in the nature of God.

Implicative Meaning of Stagnation at Mid-life: Self-Destruction

In previous pages, I have researched the meaning of generativity. This generativity produces "care" for future generations through caring for next generations, artistic works, community concerns and so on. But if mid-lifers fail to engage in this generativity in adulthood, what will happen? Erikson predicts that the result will be "stagnation."As Erikson explains the meaning of stagnation, he uses the term, "self-absorption."[60] This self-absorption is one of the polarities of adulthood. He describes the major reason of stagnation as associated with the result of previous stages as he emphasizes the importance of "cogwheeling of life cycle." In other words, stagnation is not a sudden phenomena happening in the stage of mid-life, but it is an accumulated result of previous stages. Regarding the cause of stagnation he explains as follows:

Generativity thus is an essential stage on the psychosexual as well as on the psychosocial schedule. Where such enrichment fails altogether, regression to an obsessive need for pseudo-intimacy takes place, often with a pervading sense of stagnation and personal impoverishment. Individuals, then, often, begin to indulge themselves as if they were their own-or one another's-one and only child; and where conditions favor it, early invalidism, physical or psychological becomes the vehicle of self-concern....The reasons are often to be found in early childhood impressions; in excessive self-love based on a too strenuously self-made personality; and finally(and here we return to the beginnings) in the lack of some faith, "belief in the species," which would make a child appear to be a welcome trust of the community.[61]

An unbalanced psychological development through one's life often brings out unadaptable psychological anxiety to individuals; because of this people withdraw themselves to a previous stage of conflicts.[62] When one's needs for generativity, such as the "need to be needed" and realizing the "meaning of immorality" are not met in the stage of adulthood, people fall into the core of selfish concerns. As mentioned in the previous paragraph, Erikson traces the most important cause of stagnation in mid-life back to the early childhood impressions in which people were not welcomed by their social milieu. This is what he searched for in his clinical research. And he argues that the tendencies of stagnation show two phenomena: ego-interests and libidinal investment.

It has taken psychoanalysis some time to realize that the ability to lose oneself in the meeting of bodies and minds leads to a gradual expansion of ego-interests and to a libidinal investment in that which is being generated.[63]

Regarding these ego-interests and libidinal investments he describes the phenomena of stagnation as follows:

Where generative enrichment in its various forms fails together, regression to earlier stages may occur either in the form of *an obsessive need for pseudo-intimacy* or of *a compulsive kind of preoccupation with self-imagery* - and both with a pervading sense of stagnation. Stagnation, like the antithesis in all stages, marks the potential core pathology of this stage and will, of course, involve some regression to previous conflicts. Yet it must be understood also in its stage-specific importance. This, as indicated, is especially important today when sexual frustration in recognized as pathologenic, while generative frustration, according to the dominant technological ethos of birth control, is apt to remain unrecognized.[64]

In this sense, Erikson defines the basic antipathy of stagnation as "rejectivity."[65] In other words, rejectivity implies that those who are in self-absorption have no concern and care for others, but only for themselves, because whereas generativity is a kind of altruism, self-absorption is selfish. It is a kind of narcissism concerning the meaning of life, and the reasons of existence are categorized only within "I." Don Browning points out that self-absorption is dangerous because it is not limited to one generation. Self-absorption is transmitted to the next generation. He says:

> Whatever the reasons, an inadequate capacity for generativity not only brings subtle diminishment to those who suffer from it, but it passes itself on to succeeding generations. The sins of the fathers are indeed visited upon their children and upon their children's children.[66]

In considering the meaning of stagnation Erikson indicates that a "nongenerative mentality" is the problem of modern people. The modern people do not take care of what they generate and create. We have experienced lots of instances of this, such as how parents treat their kids, destructive experiments of technology and science, destruction of the environment and so on.[67] Of course creative work, raising children, concern for community, and so on belong to the categories of generativity. But Erikson warns that if "care," which is the virtue of generativity, is not involved in those activities, it means we are accustomed to a "'nongenerative mentality." It belongs to the same category in which Erikson points out the danger of sexual intimacy without true love at the stage of young adulthood. In other words, nowadays people just make, build, or even create something for their own purpose. Even in the nongenerative mentality people know how to create and raise children, but they are not concerned about "caring." All these purposes are based on egocentricity and self-love. Creating and concerns are only for oneself. In this situation, the more people work, the more they are involved in self-absorption. The more we make something the more we feel stagnated because of the lack of care involved. To achieve our purpose we do not care for others. Achievement is a means for making modern people's meaning. By achieving and by having, we try to identify who we are. Thus, having and achieving become a general rule for measuring one's life value and meaning of life. Erikson indicates several elements which exist in modernity: pluralism, rapid social change, increased rationalization of life in the form of bureaucracy, and corporate capitalism. In these perspectives, Erikson thinks that modernity is an unfavorable ecological milieu for integrating functions of the ego, since it produces a general tendency of "uprootedness."[68]

Donald Capps's explanation regarding stagnation is helpful for understanding Erikson's explanation about stagnation. He insists that self-absorption depreciates concern for others.

> The sense of stagnation, usually accompanied by boredom and interpersonal impoverishment, often takes the form of self-indulgence....Stagnation also takes the form of self-absorption, a preoccupation with our own needs that makes it difficult to respond to the needs of others. Such self-absorption can produce a premature invalidism, either physical or psychological, which leads to increased self-concern and increased inability to care for other.[69]

This stagnation effect brings out various consequences. First of all, it destroys one's meaning of life, which is supposed to be generative. Secondly, it effects others who expected to be nurtured and cared for by generative people.[70] Lastly, as mentioned by Don Browning, stagnation/self-absorption is not finished in one generation, but is transmitted to future generations. In comparing the virtue of the seventh stage of Erikson's psychosocial theory, Donald Capps suggests the deadly sin of stagnation/self-absorption. He names it "apathy." He argues that "apathy" has various meanings, such as misery, dejection, negligence, indifference, listlessness and boredom. "Apathy," in English, is closest to the meaning of "acedia." He insists that the meaning of "acedia" is close to "indifference." By comparing these two words, he argues that "acedia"(indifference) indicates the victims of lack of interest, and "apathy" means the psychological and spiritual conditions of those who are not able to take an interest in others.[71] Thus, stagnation (self-absorption) means to fall into physical and psychological deformation. In this perspective, first stagnation alienates people from the world, and then in the second stage it becomes a self-alienation.

Thus, the most extreme case of acedia is a removal from all concerns and participation in caring for others, and then an extreme alienation from even the care for oneself. In other words, stagnation can turn out not only to destroy others but also be self-destructive. Those who are in this category refuse to undertake their own concern, caring, and good works because they think the personal sacrifice seems too high and the rewards of it too low.[72] Donald Capps divides acedia into two forms, passive and active. In the passive form, we feel the absence of hope and desire, and in the active form we experience some distortion of desires. In the passive form, without having a meaningful purpose and value in life people just live their lives. In the active form, the meaning of being, life, and value are distorted. This distorted and camouflaged meaning of life has replaced and dominated mid-lifers drives and goals. Thus "acedia" can be defined as follows:

> Acedia is the sin that believes in nothing, cares for nothing, seeks to know nothing, interferes with nothing, enjoys nothing, hates nothing, finds purpose in nothing, lives for nothing, and remains alive because there is nothing for which it will die.[73]

Stagnated people at mid-life represent those who are in narcissism in which they do not have hope or purpose of life, and are indifferent towards family, neighbors, and community. Conversely, generativity is deeply rooted in the instinctive desire to transcend and realize oneself in terms of a concern and caring for future generations, community, etc. Don Browning calls this a tendency towards "transcendence." Although we have such a desire, we also have the other side of acedia, stagnation and self-absorption. Browning calls this a "rootedness" tendency. We have a desire to transcend, but also the snare of rootedness. Humanity's limitation always blocks its desire for transcendence.[74] Human limitation, finitude, and modernity tend to compel modern people to form their life purposes, values and goals to be camouflaged by narcissistic viewpoints. Modern people have become narcissistic. Not only as individuals but also globally, in narcissistic tendencies, we are distorted inside and outside. This is the phenomena of individual and global stagnation (self-absorption). Thus, in reality, we are accustomed to stagnation and self-absorption in a vicious circle. This vicious circle is one of the worst influences that obstructs and destroys generativity. Thus, the identity of generativity in modern society is called "the spiritual problem in our time."[75] In this spiritual crisis, we may have experienced a mental deformation and it results in the disintegrity of life. There is no hope and no meaning, but only despair. Mid-life crisis in man implies an involvement in the archaic desire and the teleologic, which comes out from humanity's deep desire to be generative. It is an instinctive power which wants to experience immortality in terms of leaning our souls to God. Thus, a major concern at this moment is if culture does not provide some milieu which stimulates individuals to form a sense of generativity, what things will happen to individuals and society even though generativity is our instinctual power? A desirable milieu for individuals is to provide a cultural circumstance which encourages and enriches our inherited archaic unconsciousness for the realization of generativity.

Summary

Erik H. Erikson's psychosocial development theory is based on Epigenesis, which means the psychological growth of humans is like the development of a fetal organ system. For Erikson, the human body has its own time to grow. Similarly, human psychological potentialities have their own time to grow.[76] In this way, Erikson creates a psychosocial developmental theory which emphasizes the growth of human personality through the interaction with *soma, psyche* and *ethos* which is called "triple bookkeeping." In this perspective he sees the formation of human personality not only by epigenesis but also by social interaction.

In the formation of the polarities of adulthood in the seventh stage (generativity and stagnation), Erikson emphasizes the instinctual power of generativity in relationship with the social environment. Erikson believes that the positive side of the seventh stage, generativity, is not limited to socially or economically privileged classes, because it is a general rule. He explains that generativity has three implications: procreativity, productivity, and creativity. These three levels imply that generativity, in general, means a human instinct to leave something valuable, physically and mentally, to the next generation. Erikson refers to generativity as the "instinctual power behind various forms of selfless 'caring.'" In this instinctual power, people in adulthood/mid-life want to leave something for successive generations and community. Also there is a desire to teach something, which is creative, to the next generation. By leaving valuable/creative things to the next generation, people issue forth the meaning of life in generativity.[77]

But Erikson understands the instinctual power in relationship with social environment, because he believes that there is also a crucial element which affects self-identity. This is social force. He insists that self and identity interact in a widening radius of social relationships. Cultural changes such as family and society are regarded as essential elements to the understanding of one's process of identity.

Regarding the negative side, stagnation, Erikson explains that it brings out pseudo-intimacy or compulsive "self-absorption." What is unique to the peculiar theory of Erikson is that he argues that stagnation or generativity is an accumulated result of previous consequent stages. In other words, according to Erikson's clinical experience regarding stagnation, he discovers that major causes of stagnation are "faulty identifications with parents; in excessive self-love based on a too strenuously self-made personality; and finally in the lack of some faith, some 'belief in the species,' which would make a child appear to be a welcome trust of community."[78] In terms of showing the opposite side of generativity, Erikson emphasizes the important role of the social environment in the formation of one's identity in mid-life. In fact, we have more experiences in the process of stagnation than in that of generativity. Thus, Erikson's psychological explanation about stagnation is a key element to understanding the contemporary psychological tendency and how the social environment affects one's identity. So what Erikson's psychosocial theory implies is that the function of generativity is general, an instinctive psyche, but it functions in terms of interaction between the social environment and the instinctive psyche. In this sense, the role of the social environment, such as family, society, and school, is essential to germinate generativity at mid-life. Not only this social milieu but also successful stages of each phase are necessary to experience the meaning of generativity at mid-life. Erikson's psychosocial theory, especially regarding the concept of generativity and stagnation, has a religious and prophetic message for modern people because it implies the meaning of "homo religious."

(Notes)

1. Elliott Jaques, "Midlife Crisis" in *The Course of Life Vol 3: Adulthood and the Aging Process*, eds. Stanely I. Greenspan and George H. Pollock(National Institute of Mental Health), 4

2. Joan Berzoff, et al, *Inside Out and Outside In* (Northvale, New Jersey, London Janson: Aronson Inc., 1996), 106.
3. Joan Berzoff, op. cit., 21-22.
4. Carol Gilligan, *In a Different Voice: Psychosocial Theory and Women's Development* (MA: Harvard University Press, 1982), 6.
5. Dan P. McAdams, *The Person: An Introduction to Personality Psychology* (Orlando: Harcourt Barce College Publisher, 1994), 659.
6. Erik H. Erikson, *The Life Cycle Completed* (New York: Norton & Company, 1982) 27-28.
7. Ibid., 27.
8. Erik Erikson, *Identity and the Life Cycle* (Norton: New York & London: 1980), 53.
9. Erik Erikson, *The Life Cycle Completed* (Norton: New York & London, 1994), 25-26.
10. Erik Erikson, *Childhood and Society* (Norton: New York & London, 1963), 46.
11. Erik Erikson, *The Life Cycle Completed*, 59.
12. Erik Erikson, "The Roots of Virtue," in *The Humanist Frame*. ed. Julian Huxley (New York: Harper and Bros., 1961), 150-51.
13. Erik Erikson, *Identity: Youth and Crisis* (New York: Norton & Company, 1969), 96.
14. David M. Wulff, *Psychology of Religion* (New York: John Wiley & Sons, 1991), 399.
15. Erik Erikson, *Identity and Life Cycle*, 54.
16. Ibid.
17. Ibid. 55-6.
18. Henry Gleitman, *Basic Psychology* (New York & London: W.A. Norton & Company, University of Pennsylvania, 1987), 427.
19. Jerome Kagan & Ernest Havemann, *Psychology* (New York: Harcourt Brace Jovanovich Inc. 1980), 597.
20. Erik H. Erikson & Joan M. Erikson, "On Generativity and Identity: From a Conversation with Erik and Joan Erikson," *Harvard Educational Review*, 51:2 (1981): 269.
21. Erik Erikson, *The Life Cycle Completed*, 67.
22. Don S. Browning, *Generative Man: Psychoanalysis Perspectives* (Philadelphia: The Westminster Press, 1973), 146.
23. Ibid., 164, 181.
24. Erik Erikson, *Childhood and Society*, 267.
25. Ibid.
26. Professor of psychology at the University of Michigan.
27. John Kotre, *Outliving the Self: Generativity and the Interpretation of Lives* (Baltimore and London: The Johns Hopkins University Press, 1984), 10.
28. Ibid., 11-14.
29. Professor of human development and psychology at Northwestern University.
30. Dan P. McAdams, *The Person: An Introduction to Personality Psychology*, 762.

31. Director of Institute of Organization and Social Studies and professor of Sociology, Brinell University, England.
32. Elliott Jaques, op.cit., 4.
33. Bernace L. Neugarten, "The Awareness of Middle Age", In *Middle Age*, ed. Roger Owen (London: British Broadcasting Corporation, 1967), 64.
34. John Korte, op.cit.,10.
35. Robert J. Lifton, "The sense of Immortality: On Death and the Continuity of Life," in *Exploration in Psychohistory* (New York: Simon and Schuster, 1974), 275-76.
36. Erik H. Erikson, et al. *Vital Involvement in Old Age: The Experience of Old Age in Our Time*(New York & London: W.W. Norton & Company, 1986), 76, 82.
37. Ernest Becker, *The Denial of Death* (New York: Free Press, 1973), ix.
38. Don Browning, *Generative Man: Psychoanalytic Perspectives* (New York: Delta Press, 1975), 146.
39. He is professor of Religion and Psychological Studies at University of Chicago.
40. Erik Erikson, *Identity and the Life Cycle: Selected Papers*, Psychological Issues Monograph, Vol. I (Connecticut: International Universities Press, Inc., 1959), 97.
41. Erik Erikson, *Gandhi's Truth: On the Origins of Militant Non-violence* (New York: Norton Company, 1969), 399.
42. Erik H. Erikson, et al., *Vital Involvement in Old Age*, 74-75.
43. Erik Erikson, *The Life Cycle Completed*, 70.
44. Ibid., 67.
45. Elizabeth Hall, "A Conversation with Erik Erikson," in *Psychology Today*, (June, 1983): 26.
46. Don Browning, op. cit., 146.
47. Dan P. McAdams, *The Person,* 678.
48. Ibid.
49. Don Browning, op. cit., 146.
50. Ibid.
51. Ibid., 147.
52. Ibid.
53. Mircea Eliade, "The Sacred in the Secular World," in Cultural Hermeutics Vol. I, ed. David M. Rasmussen (Dordrecht-Holland/Boston-USA: D. Reidel Publishing Company, 1973), 101.
54. Bryan S. Rennie, *Reconstructing Eliade: Making Sense of Religion* (New York: State University of New York Press, 1996), 113.
55. Don Browning, op.cit., 205.
56. Ibid.
57. Mircea Eliade, *The Sacred and the Profane: The Nature of Religion* (New York: and London: Harvest Book Harcourt Barce, 1987), 202.
58. Eugene J. Wright, *Erikson, Identity and Religion* (New York: The Westminster Press/ Seabury Press, 1982), 173.
59. Donald Capps, *Deadly Sins and Saving Virtues* (Philadelphia: Fortress Press, 1987), 132-33.

60. Erik Erikson, *Life Cycle Completed*, 55.
61. Erik Erikson, *Childhood and Society*, 267.
62. Erik Erikson, *The Life Cycle Completed*, 60.
63. Erik Erikson, *Childhood and Society*, 267.
64. Erik Erikson, *The Life Cycle Completed*, 68.
65. Ibid., 33.
66. Don Browning, op.cit.,163.
67. Ibid., 164.
68. Ibid., 169.
69. Donald Capps, op.cit., 59.
70. Ibid.
71. Ibid., 60.
72. Ibid.
73. Ibid., 61.
74. Don Browning, op. cit.,168.
75. Dan P. McAdams, op. cit., 767.
76. Erik H. Erikson, *The Life Cycle Completed*, 27-28.
77. Ibid., 81, 161
78. Erik Erikson, *Identity and the Life Cycle*, 103,104.

Chapter 3

Daniel Levinson's Research and Theory on Male Mid-life Identity

Life Cycle and Mid-life

Levinson's understanding of life cycle is that the development of life is not finished by the early stages of childhood or adolescence, but continually grows throughout one's life.[1] He believes that there is an interaction between individuals and the world and by this interaction the process of adult development continues. To understand a man's life Levinson indicates three parts which are inevitable elements. The first element is the sociocultural world which includes family, religion, class, ethnicity, vocation, and the political system. The second is understanding a man's conflicts, anxieties, and wishes which can be expressed through the man's consciousness and unconsciousness. The third is to examine and understand the man's degree of participation in his society. In other words, knowing one's transactions between the self and world is the third element.[2]

> Middle age is usually regarded as a vague interim period, defined primarily in negative terms. One is no longer young and yet not quite old - but what is one in a more positive sense? The connotations of youth are vitality, growth, mastery, the heroic; whereas old age connotes vulnerability, withering, ending, the brink of nothingness. Our overly negative imagery of old age adds greatly to the burden of middle age. It is terrifying to go through middle age in the shadow of death, as though one were already very old; and it is self-defeating illusion to live it in the shadow of youth, as though one were still simply young.[3]

Thus, Levinson researches the stages of adulthood based on three elements: changes in biological and psychological functioning, the sequence of generations, and evolving careers and enterprises.[4] In order to do research about men's life cycles, especially in adulthood, he and his associates interviewed 40 men from various jobs: ten blue collar workers, ten novelists, ten executives and ten biologists. As a result, he concluded that approximately 80% of men have suffered the mid-life crisis and that the mid-life transition (age 40-45) brings a new set of developmental tasks.[5]

As Levinson explains the cause of mid-life crisis, he relates it to two major causes: the external milieu and the self. In this sense, mid-life crisis is a result of compounding the two elements. He believes that man in this crisis is shown as somewhat irrational, upset, and sick. The problem in this mid-life crisis is pathology which interrupts the improvement of one's life.[6]

He thinks that the process of discovering the real meaning of one's life at mid-life is not an intellectual process, because it involves "emotional turmoil, despair, the sense of not knowing where to, turn to of being stagnant and unable to move at all."[7] Because of the pathological anxiety and guilt, men at mid-life often make false starts.[8] He describes false directions and, simultaneously, genuine directions for overcoming the mid-life crisis. As he mentions the genuine directions he points out that the genuine reappraisal should bring some agony because it delves into and challenges illusions formulated during the first half of life. Levinson also indicates the reason for pain in the mid-life crisis. According to him, first of all, there are some parts of the self which have been neglected or emphasized through one's life stages. Among these the neglected parts of the self want to express themselves, and people experience these as "other voices in other rooms." So during mid-life crisis people need to listen carefully to the other neglected voices.[9]

Mid-life Transition

A brief look at Levinson's theory of adulthood reveals the following stages: 1) The Early Adult Transition: This stage begins at age 17 and ends at 22. Two main functions in this period are to determine childhood periods and to prepare for entrance into early adulthood. 2)

The First Adult Life Structure: The group 22 to 28 belongs in this period. Providing a workable link between the valued self and the adult society is a chief task in this phase. Two main latent tasks are to explore the possibilities for adult living and to make something of one's life. 3) The Age Thirty Transition: This extends from 28 to 33 and provides one with an opportunity to work on the limitations and the flaws of the first jobs in this period. One attempts to have a secure place in society, and to be a valued member in his field. Another task is to seek a better life for oneself. 4) The Second Adult Life Structure: This period continues from the age thirty transition to about age 40; through this period, a man is supposed to realize his youthful aspirations. Also a man seeks the most important things in order to outlive himself in structures such as work, family and community. The Mid-life Transition: This phase lasts from age 40 to 45, and brings new questions. "What have I done for myself and others?" "Is this what I wanted?" These kinds of questions are about the meaning of life. These phenomena do not happen to all men, but a great majority of men experience them. These men struggle within the self and with the external world.[10] At this stage mid-lifers need to pass through three major tasks, which he identifies in his research. The first task is to finish up the period of early adulthood.[11] What is needed in this stage is a reappraisal of one's life structure. One's past life structure cannot be taken for granted. Levinson describes the questions regarding the reappraisal of the past.

> What have I done with my life? What do I really get from and give to my wife, children, friends, work, community-and self? What is it I truly want for myself and others? What are my greatest talents and how am I using (or wasting) them? What have I done with my early dream and what do I want with it now? Can I live in a way that combines my current desires, values and talents?[12]

As people reflects their past they need to realize life is based on illusion; this is helpful to most people during early adulthood, during which an individual's abilities and drives are maximized. But he points out that the best way to be dis-illusioned is not to want too much.[13] The second task is to take a step toward the beginning of middle adulthood. In other words, mid-lifers at the mid-life transition need to change the structure of early adulthood in order to create an appropriate structure for middle adulthood.[14] The third task is to examine the four polarities of mid-life crisis: young/old, destruction/creation, masculine/feminine, and attachment/separateness. Levinson calls this process individuation.[15] He sees that there are three individuation opportunities during one's life stages: infancy, pubescence and the mid-life transition. Through these three process people are supposed to expand their relationship toward the true self and to the world.[16]

Four Tasks of Mid-life Individuation

Why is the man supposed to ask ontological and meaningful questions regarding his past life and future life in his mid-life? Levinson points out that the reason is related to four polarities which male mid-lifers have to pass through for mid-life: Young/Old polarity, Destruction/Creation polarity, Masculine/Feminine polarity, and Attachment/Separateness polarity. Although these four polarities vary according to individuals, all individuals have these as archetypes.[17] This is what Levinson concludes from his research. And he believes that the most important thing in male mid-life is to deal carefully and successfully with these polarities. But among these archetypes Levinson thinks that the polarity of the old and young archetype is the most influential one in the mid-life transition, because it affects all three other archetypes.[18] I will explain it in detail after showing Levinson's theories about the other three archetypes. Levinson argues that the Destruction/Creation polarity is due to the conscious or unconscious realization about one's fate regarding death and impending death to others. The idea of mortality brings out two tendencies: destruction and creativity. Regarding destruction Levinson renders its cause to be the recognition of one's own mortality. And, simultaneously, the mid-lifer feels that he has a strong desire to be a creative person for himself and others, because of his awareness of his mortality. In this sense, men at mid-life experience two contrasting intentions which are the creative and the destructive.

> His growing recognition of his own mortality makes him more aware of destruction as universal process. Knowing that his own death is not far off, he is eager to affirm life for himself and for the generations to come. He wants to be more creative. The creative impulse is not merely to "make" something. It is to bring something into being, to give birth, to generate life...[19]

So a given task to mid-lifers is to sublimate the Destruction tendency to the Creativity tendency in a new way.[20] As the answer to this archetype Levinson suggests that the best way is not to give up because of destructiveness, but to live better with this polarity.[21]

Regarding the Masculine/Feminine polarity Levinson states that there are biological potentials to be a male or a female from the start of life. Only after a fetus grows up does it develop as male or female.[22] The given task of male mid-lifers in the polarity of Masculine/Feminine is to allow feminine facets, such as intimacy, to develop, and to reintegrate the Masculine/Feminine polarity.[23]

The polarity of Attachment/Separateness means to reflect on one's first half of life which sought possessions, that is seeking "having" rather than "being," based on different perspectives. Levinson mentions that Attachment belongs to the first half of life, and Separateness belongs to the second half of life. In other words, mid-lifers need to reflect on their living patterns of the past in terms of spiritual perspectives in the second half of life. Levinson calls it "Separateness." Concerning separateness, mid-lifers need to care for the development of the self.[24]

Young/Old Archetype: the Major Polarity

Among the four polarities, Levinson considers that the Young/Old polarity, which is regarded as an archetype, is the most central.[25] In describing the Young/Old polarity, Levinson defines that it is not categorized by a particular age group but by all ages. Although it occurs in all age groups, the influence of this polarity is most influential at male mid-life, because male mid-lifers begin to realize their finitude and experience death both directly and indirectly.[26]

The Young archetype represents growth, possibility, oneness, etc., whereas the Old archetype implies death, structure, completion, etc. The Young also shows fragility and impulsiveness whereas the Old imbibes tyranny, impotence and senility.[27]

But this symbol of the Young/Old archetype is experienced as related to the realization of mortality and immortality of mid-lifers. Levinson points out why mid-lifers feel acutely aware of their sense of "mortality." First of all, he indicates that as mid-lifers become old they experience intensively the probability of losses, such as the lose of strength and the death of parents, compared to the other stages of life. In other words, normally, as mid-lifers enter the stage of transition (crisis), they experience directly or indirectly the increase of others' suffering and death. In this sense, men at age 40 should realize and feel move that they will die than in any other age.[28] In other words, mid-lifers at this stage have been challenged by "loss of youth" through which they experience the decline of bodily and psychological powers. As they experience it they realize that they are mortal.[29]

In this perspective, Levinson indicates that the Young archetype means "immortality" and the Old archetype means "death." Levinson's ideas are supported by his research. He argues that the cause of mid-life crisis is due to "immortality" which is rooted in the Young archetype. In other words, realizing one's immanent death causes mid-lifers to sublimate it to the Young archetype. So immorality has become one's vitality for life.

> Why should the recognition of our mortality be so painful? Why can we not come to know it and accept it?...A primary reason, I believe, is the wish for immortality. This is one of the strongest and least malleable of human motives. It operates with great force during early adulthood as an aspect of the Young archetype...At mid-life, the growing recognition of mortality collides with the powerful wish for immortality and the many illusions that help to maintain it.[30]

In its integration of the four polarities, Levinson's theory emphasizes that male mid-life crisis is saliently associated with the fear of mortality and the desire for immortality. In other words, mid-life crisis or transition is strongly connected with the concept of death. Levinson thinks that in the mid-life crisis men know that they are close to death. The most significant experience in mid-life is death, and the concept of death is the most influential element for one's individuation. As a man in this mid-life transition begins to realize that his own mortality is not located far away from him, but close to him, he understands that death/destruction is an inevitable universal process. Based on this truth, he begins to be more creative. To be a creative being means to be a meaningful being.[31] Death reminds us of the destruction of all things that we have developed, achieved and created, but, simultaneously, it stimulates us to be meaningful and creative beings while we live the second half of life. To Levinson the mid-life crisis is a stage for the development of psychological progress.[32]

Regarding the influence of death on male mid-lifers, Elliott Jaques's[33] research on the relationship between mid-life crisis and death supports strongly Levinson's research on the focus of Young and Old polarity of mid-life crisis. Jaques researched 310 artists' biographical information and artistic productions. Among them were Mozart, Shakespeare, Michelangelo, and Raphael. What Jaques found is that before the age of 40, their works, themes, and concerns were about romance and passion. With pure desire and romance, they expressed their art in a passionate way. Before the age of 40, they were filled with some optimistic view of life. But after the age of 40, their themes and concerns changed. With an increasing concern about death, mortality became an artistic concern along with a pessimistic view of life. After age 40, their works developed contemplative pessimism, and were expressed in more philosophical and ontological language.[34] He found that most genius artists experienced actual death by the age of 37. Based on this research Jaques insists that the male mid-life crisis begins in the late thirties and that the mid-life crisis is considered to be a transition which can be continued from around forty to even the late fifties.[35] He describes the psychological tendencies of mid-life as follows:

> Forty is a noticeably restless, introspective, morose, moody, peevish, and melancholy person. When asked to describe his life, Forty will reply vaguely that it is "awful," or "depression," without being able to say exactly why. Thirty is satisfied with familiar surroundings and content to play with his own toys. Not so Forty, who instead is continually on the lookout for greener pastures and who spends much of his time day-dreaming about running away with someone who really appreciates him. Forty tends to be morbidly convinced that he is very sick (brain cancer and heart trouble are two especially favored diagnosis), and grieves over the degeneration, both real and imagined, of his physical and mental capacities. It is not too much to say that Forty manages to make life miserable for those who must live with him, possibly because he seems unable to live with himself.[36]

Because of psychological changes in mid-life Jaques concludes that the mid-life crisis can be expressed in three different ways.

> This crisis may express itself in three different ways: The creative career may simply come to an end, either in a drying up of creative work or in actual death; the creative capacity may begin to show and express itself for the first time; or a decisive change in the quality and content of creativeness may take place.[37]

The turning point at around age forty provides middle aged men with special meaning: I have lived a half of my life and another half is waiting for me. If I use another half, then what will be waiting for me? To those who are in this period, it is a time to think of existential and inner questions, such as: What am I here for? What do I have to do for the rest of my life? What is left to look forward to? In this process, people who are in mid-life also develop new concepts of time. Forty cuts the life span neatly in two. In this sense mid-life is called the "half-way mark," the "point of the great divide," and the "frightening pivot point between the up and down of life."[38] Now the middle aged person faces the double-edged sword of time. One edge appears as a prod, and the other appears as a brake. These concepts of time cause people to think of how much pleasure can be obtained in their remaining time; how many years are left for the final stage, and how many activities can be undertaken.[39] All of these mixed feelings regarding life pushes people to think of death, which was once considered as superficial, as a reality. But at about age forty, life and death are no longer unrelated. Elliott Jaques (1965) says in his article "the Mid-Life Crisis and Death;"

> Family and occupation have become established; parents have grown old, and children are at the threshold of adulthood. Youth and childhood are past and gone, and demand to be mourned. The achievement of mature and independent adulthood presents itself as the main psychological task. The paradox is that of entering the prime of life, while the stages of fulfillment are dated. Death lies beyond... I believe, and shall try to demonstrate that it is this fact, the entry upon one's psychological scene of the reality and inevitability of one's own personal death, that is the central and crucial feature of the mid-life phase - the feature which precipitates the critical nature of the period.[40]

Jaques argues that the instinct of death is influential whether men know about it or not, or even deny it, because this instinct of death, unconsciousness, is associated with the infantile unconscious relationship to death. Infantile unconsciousness implies the infant's instinct to survive in terms of attaching to the primary caregivers against the threat of fear and death. And this infantile unconsciousness appears in creative ways as ideas of immortality during mid-life crisis.

> ...whether he can face this reality, or whether he denies it - will be markedly influenced by his infantile unconscious relation to death, a relationship which depends upon the stage and nature of the working through of the infantile depressive position, as Klein (1948, 1955)...Ideas of immortality arise as a response to these anxieties and as a defense against them. Unconscious fantasies of immortality are the counterpart of the infantile of the indestructible and hence immortal aspect of the idealized and bountiful primal object.[41]

Most males who are in mid-life enjoy something of a culmination of the growth, development and productivities of the earlier years or experience a restlessness and dissatisfaction within. Realization, fulfillment or disappointment is intensified during this period. In this period death is not considered to be the loss of someone else, but as one's own death; that is personal and actual mortality. One is living one's life more towards death at this phase than out of youth. In this sense the last half of life, mid-life, can be and usually is lived in conscious knowledge of eventual death as part of one's daily life.[42] Daniel Levinson also mentions the influence of death in mid-life.[43]

In the realization of their morality at middle age, men want to bequeath material, products, value, etc., to future generations, community and society. All these things imply the ultimate value of one's life through one's experiences. This desire to leave some valuable things is called "legacy." Of course, "legacy" is different according to each individual and it is impossible to measure it. But it is the ultimate of value in one's life.

> In every era, a man normally has the need and the capability to generate a legacy. But in the Mid-life Transition the meaning of legacy deepens and the task of building a legacy acquires its greatest developmental significance. As we learn better how to foster development in adulthood, "creating a legacy" will become an increasingly important part of middle adulthood. This will add both to the personal fulfillment of individual adults and to the quality of life for succeeding generations.[44]

In other words, comparing mid-lifers with other age groups, mid-lifers want to bequeath their essential meanings to their descendants or community, because in this way they can outlive their own selves through others. Levinson believes that this tendency is the intention of mid-lifers who want to live forever.[45]

Not only this concern for posterity but also concern for religious institutions, the community, college, professional society, charity and helping worthy things reflects one's desire to create a legacy for a future generation which is upgraded in quality and quantity.[46] This tendency at mid-life can manifest in a teacher, reliever, healer and mentor. All these thoughts and behaviors occur the most efficiently and strongly at mid-life even though these tendencies can happen in all age groups. And Levinson believes that all these roles are associated with altruism, and this altruism is "a vehicle for the search for immortality."[47]

Levinson points out that immortality through which mid-lifers seek their legacy implies humanity's desire to seek the eternal soul. This tendency throughout human history and civilization cannot be forgotten, because it is a human instinct. Levinson thinks that this desire to live forever is rooted in "the archetypes of the Young and the Self as eternal figures."[48] But an emerging problem in this human tendency is the consequence of destructiveness because of external milieus such as education, family, and society.[49] In this sense Levinson indicates that to experience this legacy at least two elements need to be satisfied: passing successfully through the four polarities, and good enough development through one's life stages.[50] The concept of "good-enough" can be explained by saying that mothers cannot be perfect care-givers for their infants, but that "good-enough mothering" is enough to nurture an infant.[51] As such this good-enough development through life stages is important for going through male mid-life identity.

Levinson and his associates conclude that the major cause of the mid-life crisis is the fear of mortality, which raises questions about the triviality, meaninglessness, and hopelessness of life.[52] Contemporary middle-aged adults have been more affected psychologically than the middle-aged adults of any other era since the expected age of humans is increasing. In this sense mortality comes slowly to contemporary people. These extended periods of life, plus the convenience of modern living, give us lots of time to think about what death is. We have more time, as it were, to think over death and life than persons at any other age in history. In a word, the most powerful influence or change during the mid-life transition is the intensifying awareness that one's life is limited to a finite number of years. This change in thinking gives some the realization that each person should attempt a meaning-making process, giving life depth and meaning. The awareness of fear about the unknown world after life, death, is the main cause for the mid-life crisis even though death itself may not yet be an immediate problem to the middle-aged. In confronting the potential fear of death at mid-life what a mid-lifer can do is "create a legacy." In this terms, men can sublimate their fear to altruism and can experience satisfaction through bequeathing valuable legacy to future generations and to society. But what is important to pass through this mid-life crisis is to have "good enough" development which can develop successively the archetypes of polarity.[53]

(Notes)

1. Daniel Levinson, et al., *The Seasons of a Man's Life* (New York: Ballantine Books, 1978), 195.
2. Ibid., 42.

3. Ibid., preface. X
4. Ibid., 27-30.
5. Ibid., 199.
6. Ibid.
7. Ibid.
8. Ibid.
9. Ibid, 200.
10. Ibid., 56-62.
11. Ibid., 191.
12. Ibid., 192.
13. Ibid., 193.
14. Ibid., 194
15. Ibid., 197.
16. Ibid., 195.
17. Ibid., 196-97 & 209.
18. Ibid., 209-21.
19. Ibid., 222.
20. Ibid., 197 & 222-28.
21. Ibid., 223.
22. Ibid., 228.
23. Ibid., 235-36.
24. Ibid., 241-43.
25. Ibid., 209.
26. Ibid., 194.
27. Ibid., 209-10.
28. Ibid., 215.
29. Ibid., 213-14.
30. Ibid., 215-16.
31. Ibid., 222.
32. Ibid., 26, 196.
33. Elliott Jaques has M.D., Ph. D., F.R.C. Psych. He is director of Institute of Organization and Social Studies and professor of Sociology, Brinell University, England.
34. Elliott Jaques, "Midlife Crisis" in *The Course of Life* (Vol. III): *Adulthood and the Aging Process*, eds. Stanley I. Greenspan & George H. Pollock (Maryland: National Institute of Mental Health, 1981), 8.
35. Ibid., 2.
36. Elliott Jaques, "The Midlife Crisis" in *Forty*, ed. Stanley Brandes(Knoxville: The University of Tennessee Press), 24.
37. Ibid., 4.
38. Ibid., 27.
39. Ibid.

40. Elliott Jaques, "The Mid-Life and Death," In *International Journal of Psychoanalysis*, No 4 (1965):506.
41. Elliott Jaques, "Midlife Crisis," in *The Course of Life* (Vol III), 12-13.

42. Elliott Jaques, "The Midlife Crisis" in *Forty*, 32.
43. Daniel Levinson, op. cit., 26.
44. Ibid., 221.
45. Ibid., 219.
46. Ibid.
47. Ibid.
48. Ibid., 221.
49. Ibid.
50. Ibid., 218-221.
51. Donald Winnicott, "Ego Distortion in Terms of True and False Self," in *The Maturational Processes and the Facilitating Environment* (Madison, Connecticut: International Universities Press, 1966), 140-52.
52. Daniel Levinson, op. cit., preface.
53. Ibid., 197-221.

PART II

Paul Tillich and the Theology of the Male Self at Mid-life

Chapter 4

Paul Tillich's Theological Interpretation on the Self

Theological Interpretation on the Self

I have researched the psychological meaning of male mid-life crisis in the preceding chapters. All psychological researches on male mid-life are deeply associated with the identity of the self at mid-life. So I tend to analyze "the self" in Tillich's theological perspective in this part, because Tillich's theological concept of "the centered self" can provide a theological dialogue on the male self at mid-life. Another reason for examining Tillich is his theological understanding about human situations and predicaments which gives theological and psychological implications for understanding the entire character of the self.

Tillich's theological methodology is a "correlational methodology" in which message and situation are related. He uses this methodology through his book *Systematic Theology*. There are two purposes of his systematic theology. The first is to bring the statement of the Christian message, and the second is to interpret the Christian message to each generation.[1] In this perspective, Tillich calls his theology the apologetic theology. He thinks that "it correlates questions and answers, situation and message, human existence and divine manifestation."[2] In other words, first of all, he begins to talk about human situations and questions through an anthropological approach. Hence, Tillich's theology starts not with God, but with humans. In this sense, he regards that theology must be considered the "answering theology" for human situations.[3] In this same vein, in order to understand the estranged situations of human beings, Tillich suggests how much the dialogue between depth psychology and theology is needed as follows:

> Now how are theological judgments applied to depth psychology and existentialism(which are in reality one thing). The relation between man's essential nature and his existential predicament is the first and basic question that theology has asked whenever it encounters existentialist analyses and psychoanalytic material.[4]

So, Tillich's theological methodology can give us a number of tools for analyzing and understanding the anxieties for the self at mid-life, and provides us with a basis for pastoral reflection in terms of his theological understandings about the self and God.

The Centered Self as the Image of God

According to Tillich humans are the only beings aware of the structure of being because they have 'the self' structure. In talking about the definition of the self, Tillich emphasizes its originality, comparing all other things with the self.[5] Essentially, the self exists before all questions of existence. In this perspective it is impossible to think about "what are human beings?" without knowing "what is the self?" He regards the self as the center in which people experience that they are the center of themselves and the world. In other words, human beings are the only fully centered beings, because we have complete centeredness.[6] This complete centeredness provides human beings with greatness and dignity through which they reveal potentiality as the center brings together themselves and the world. In this point, Tillich names the centered self "the image of God," and as "true being."[7] Thus, the original meaning of the self plays a crucial role in understanding what the human being is in Tillich's theology. Because of the crucial importance of the self Tillich emphasizes that essentially the self belongs to the divine center.[8] But, despite the fact that the self as the image of God has plenty of potentiality, why is it hard to experience such potentialities through the self? We have experienced and heard about personal and global sufferings such as regional wars, racial and religious conflicts, domestic violence, ecological crisis, family sufferings, etc. We cannot stop asking this question repeatedly. Most of these phenomena are due to people's inflated self and individualism which blind and close their minds so that they are absorbed in their narcissistic deteriorating world. This is the tragic truth of the human self. Tillich articulates the reason for human tragedy. First of all he indicates that the possibilities of the self as true being and the image of God implies two things: perfection and temptation. As the centered self realizes the potentialities of itself through itself and the world, human beings are tempted to make it as the center of themselves and the world, because human beings are not bound to any situations.[9] As people practice their freedom in terms of temptation, they experience the estranged self. In this sense Tillich believes that human beings are existentially estranged from the divine center. This means that human beings are estranged from the ground of being, which results in personal guilt, universal misery, and our estrangement from ourselves, others and God.[10] In describing the meaning of existential estrangement Tillich shows three elements which contradict the created structure of a human being: unbelief, hubris and concupiscence.[11] These three elements are regarded as the marks of human estrangement.[12] For this reason the human self has experienced self-contradiction which drives toward self-destruction in order to annihilate individuals and the whole. But Tillich's theological understanding regarding the self can give two meanings for the healing of the self at mid-life. To clarify our understanding of the self in Tillich's theology we need to understand estrangement.

> Man as he exists is not what he essentially is and ought to be. He is estranged from his true being. The profundity of the term "estrangement" lies in the implication that one belongs essentially to that from which one is estranged. Man is not a stranger to his true being, for he belongs to it. He is judged by it but cannot be completely separated, even if he is hostile to it. Man's hostility to God provides indisputably that he belongs to him. Where there is the possibility of hate, there and there alone is the possibility of love.[13]

First, we need to understand the human predicament in terms of a theological understanding of human estrangement which results in alienation from God, others and oneself, in terms of self-loss or self-elevation.[14] The representative characteristics of human estrangement mentioned previously, "unfaith," "hubris," and "concupiscence," which have been regarded as universal traits in Tillich's theology,[15] can provide some understanding of how the fundamental problems of the self at mid-life happen. Secondly, the implication of the previous paragraph is that we human beings live in "estrangement" in which we have become alienated from the essentials of being human. But this does not mean that we are strangers to true beings or the centered self, because we essentially belong to it but not existentially. In this sense Tillich insists that we are not completely separated from the ground of being.[16] As long as we exist as human beings it is inevitable to say that the origin of human beings comes from the divine center and we still keep the image of God.

Self-Estrangement as Unbelief

Tillich describes the meaning of "unbelief" in the perspective of the Protestant Church and St. Augustine. In the perspective of Tillich, "unbelief" is regarded as separation of human will from God's will. It is an act or stage of total separation from God. In this sense, he insists that "unbelief" is " the act of total personality which includes practical, theoretical and emotional facts. Thus "unbelief" is the human "estrangement from God in the center of his being."[17] Why do we have such a tendency? The reason is that it is the tendency of the self to have the pleasure of a separated life, keeping away from divine blessedness. In this process of seeking of self-absorption for the existential self-realization, human beings only concentrate on themselves and their world, which causes them to lose the ground of the self and the world.[18]

Finally, this tendency of human beings results in their estrangement not only from God but also from the center of their being. Tillich points out concretely the estrangement of "unbelief" in three perspectives: knowledge (cognition), will (law) and emotion (love).[19] This self-centeredness of the human self comes from human nature which wants to possess every finite thing as a manifestation of the infinite.

Self-Estrangement as Hubris

The reason that humans can be estranged or self-elevated is based on the structure of the human in which they are the only conscious, self-conscious and completely centered beings. In other words, this peculiarity of human beings gives us greatness and dignity. It is regarded as one of peculiarities of the image of God in Tillich's theology.[20] This greatness of the self in humanity makes human beings transcend the self and the world, because the capacity of human beings induces people to challenge all things from the perspective of the center. In this sense, Tillich thinks that the self is rooted in the divine center.[21] But this capacity of human beings brings temptation. Because of this human potentiality only human beings have the image of God. But this greatness of human beings drives toward "hubris." And if the human self does not acknowledge its limitations, Tillich says, we fall into "hubris," because the human self elevates oneself beyond the limit of one's finite category. As Tillich explains the meaning of hubris, he compares it with the story of Eve and the serpent in Genesis. In other words, human beings are seduced continually to judge and consider our potentiality as unlimitedness. In this situation we experience self-elevation through which we are buried in oblivion about human limitations. For this reason, the human self knows one's freedom but does not acknowledge one's destiny. And this tendency of hubris can appear through humility or self-elevation because it is the universality of human beings.

> It is most distinctly expressed in the serpent's promise to Eve that eating from the tree of knowledge will make man equal to God. *Hubris* is the self-elevation of man into the sphere of the divine. Man is capable of such self-elevation because of his greatness....The greatness of man lies in his being infinite, and it is just this temptation of *hubris* into which he universally falls through destiny and freedom...*Hubris* is not the special quality of man's moral character. It is universally human; it can appear in acts of humility as well as in acts of pride. Although it is possible to enlarge the meaning of pride to include *hubris*, it seems to be less confusing to use the term "self-elevation" for *hubris*.[22]

Self-elevation is the root of all kinds of human evil and this phenomena is considered a universal phenomenon in Tillich's theology. The tendency to be the center for one's self and one's world is universal. Based on this fact no one is willing to accept one's finitude. If one is ready to accept one's limitations, it means that one will manifest another type of hubris.[23]

Self-Estrangement as Concupiscence

When Tillich defines the definition of "unbelief" as removing one's self from the divine center, and "hubris" as making oneself the center of oneself and of one's world, he raises a question concerning why human beings are tempted to be the center in themselves. Regarding his own questions he answers as follows:

> The question naturally arises concerning why man is tempted to become centered in himself. The answer is that it places him in the position of drawing the whole of his world into himself. It elevates him beyond his particularity and makes him universal on the basis of his particularity.[24]

If so, why do human beings want to place themselves at the center of the self and the world? Regarding this question Tillich answers that because we are separated from the whole we want to reunite with the whole. And this lack of perfection makes people search for abundance. This tendency to seek total satisfaction is called "concupiscence" in Tillich's theology.[25]

The scope of "concupiscence" is varied and includes such desires as physical hunger, sex, knowledge, power, material wealth and spiritual values. "Concupiscence," is not only limited to sexual boundaries, but also all areas of human life. Because of this we are endlessly seeking satisfaction for these things, for we desire the union with the whole. If it is categorized in a specific area such as sex, "concupiscence" cannot be used to describe the general state of estrangement. From this point of view "concupiscence" implies one's insatiable and incessant relations to one's world and to one's self.[26] This human tendency appears throughout history. Tillich illustrates several examples through Kierkegaard's interpretation, such as Emperor Nero who embodied unlimited power and brought death to whatever he encountered, the figure of Mozart's Don Juan, the seducer who was possessed with unlimited sexual striving, and the figure of Goethe's Faust who accepted the pact with the devil in order to know everything. In addition to these examples Tillich illustrates two others: Sigmund Freud's definition of "libido" and Nietzsche's "will to power." Tillich believes that Freud's theory of "libido" shows humans' unlimited desire to release sexual tension and points out our "discontent" with our creativity. But Tillich indicates that Freud's interpretation of libido is not sufficient to reinterpret the meaning of concupiscence, because, theologically speaking, Freud did not see humans' essential nature but existential nature. In Tillich's perspective, libido is not regarded as concupiscence because, in essence, libido is love which is to be united with the other qualities of love such as *eros, philia,* and *agape*.[27] Thus Tillich insists that there is a salient difference between love as *libido* and love as *concupiscence*.[28]

Regarding the concept of Nietzsche's "will to power" Tillich interprets it neither as a conscious psychological act nor as an act of power to control human against human. Because this desire is based on the essential human desire to express one's power of being, it needs to be understood in terms not only of existential desire but also of essential desire.[29] In describing these things as they appear in existentialist literature, psychology, art and philosophy, Tillich suggests that all these tendencies come from the human desire to put the universe into one's self.[30]

In conclusion, as Tillich explains the three categories of self-estrangement, which are regarded as universal human traits, "unbelief," "hubris," and "concupiscence," he interprets these elements as bringing human destruction and self-elevation. He states that these human tendencies appear destructively in human contexts. In terms of this self-elevation we are totally estranged from God, others, and ourselves. But Tillich's analysis of the human self does not stop at this point but points out human ontological desire associated with self-elevation. In other words, Tillich believes that all these desires reflect the essential human desire to return to the center of the whole, God. All these concepts imply how much human beings desire to be reunited with the centered self which is expressed as the archetypal image of God in Jung's psychology.[31] Tillich believes that all these human predicaments do not reflect what humans essentially are and ought to be, but points out how much we are eager to be reunited with the centered self/ the divine self.[32]

The Self-Loss and the World-loss as the Loss of Determining Self

Through the three universal estrangements of the self, "unbelief," "hubris," and "concupiscence," human beings find that they are in existential estrangement which contradicts the essential human quality of potentiality for goodness.[33] This estrangement of human beings contradicts the created self and the world, and it drives self-destruction which destroys not only oneself but also the whole. In this sense, Tillich argues that this destruction is not due to external forces but is the result of the structure of estrangement.[34] In other words, the destruction of non-being is always related to being, because non-being works based on being. Self-destruction cannot occur without being itself.[35]

Tillich indicates that self-loss because of self-estrangement leads to the loss of a determining center for oneself. The loss of one's determining center implies the disintegration of the centered self because of disruptive drives. These disruptive drives replace the centered self and threaten to split the person, which results in the destruction of unity. In terms of this process, people experience the destruction of the centered self and loss of the world. We can experience the results of self-destruction in our moral conflicts and psychopathology. Furthermore, in this situation, things no longer have a right relation to people because people lose the centered self and lose the power to encounter by things as meaningful.[36] In other words, in this case, all things encountered with the self can control the self because it lost power. As people lose the centered self they lose the power to control things, which means they become slaves to things. Things can have control over people because of the loss of the centered self.[37]

Self-loss brings out the loss of centered self for human beings, and it makes people be limited selves which only depend on their environment, because these people have lost their world. Thus the loss of the centered self, comparing it with the environment, means that people are bound by their environment.[38] In this sense, as people lose the centered self they become slaves to things, which control human minds because we are too much captured in them. We can no longer regard each other as beings but as things.

In conclusion, the implication of Tillich's analysis of self-loss is that it is intimately associated with the phenomena of stagnation in the male mid-life crisis. Some male mid-lifers experience the scattered self which is the result of losing the centered self. Tillich's following words reflect his theological analysis of this phenomena.

> Self-loss is the loss of one's determining center, the disintegration of the unity of the person. This is manifest in moral conflicts and in psychopathological disruptions, independently or interdependently. The horrifying experience of "falling to pieces" gets hold of the person. To the degree in which this happens, one's world also falls to pieces. It ceases to be a world, in the sense of meaningful whole.[39]

As we experience self-loss at mid-life we experience the disintegration of our lives, because in terms of self-loss the meaning of life is "falling to pieces." All environments which we experience do not bear any meaning because of losing our centered self. In this sense this theological reflection on self-loss gives insights as to what the major cause of male mid-life crisis is and how can we overcome this crisis in terms of recovering the centered self.

The Actualization of the Self: Ontological Polarities of the Self

Tillich argues that the phenomena of self-loss and self-estrangement apparently appear in "the interdependent loss of the polar elements of being."[40] Tillich thinks of life as the process of actualization of potential being. And this actualization is realized throughout all of the life process. It denotes a movement out from a center, which is the essential axis and root.[41] But Tillich points out an inseparable relationship between the self and the world for the actualization of the self. He calls it the subject-object structure.

In talking about the self, Tillich notes that the self exists prior to all things. So he states that the self is "the original phenomenon which precedes all questions of existence."[42] But, in spite of the self being the centering power through which actions and reactions occur, it is influenced by the interaction between the self and the world. So human beings are not separated beings. It is impossible to think about humanity without considering the social interaction between the self and the world. In other words, the action of the self is grounded in the dialectical process of self-identity, self-alteration, and return to the self. This forms the basic functions of life for the realization of being. Through this process the potentialities of the self become actuality which we call life. And each of the three is reflected the ontological polarities of the self.[43]

> The basic structure of self-identity and self-alteration is effective in each, and each is dependent on the basic polarities of being: self-integration on the polarity of individualization and participation, self-creation on the polarity of dynamics and form, self-transcendence on the polarity of freedom and destiny.[44]

Tillich believes that this structure of the life process leads to self-integration, the first function of life which is the process of self-identity. Self-integration is the nature of life and life expresses itself through self-integration in the life process.[45] But the self-actualization of life does not stay in only self-integration but move back to the center. And this process is called the self-alteration. Through this process the self produces new centers through which it creates the horizontal direction. The reason for producing new directions in the horizontal directions is that life always drives toward the new which is, of course, based on the centered self but it drives toward the new in terms of transcending the centered self. Tillich ascribes the cause of creativity of life to life itself, because creative power is given to life.[46] The third direction of the centered self is the vertical direction, which contrasts to the horizontal direction, the self-transcending function. Whereas self-integration and self-creation mean the function of the self within the limit of the finite, self-transcendence means to go beyond the finite life. In this sense, it is called "driving toward the sublime."[47] All these three functions of life are crucial to understanding the peculiarities of the self, so I will now turn to an exploration of them.

The Self-Integration and Its Ambiguity: Individualization and Participation

The first polarity of the self in the structure of being is individuation and participation. These two elements appear through the function of self-integration in terms of the principle of centeredness. In this sense "centeredness" is the quality of individuation. Thus, Tillich points out that a fully individualized being is, simultaneously, a fully centered being. This individualization is the given privilege to only human beings, whereas, to other beings, centeredness and individualization are partially limited and fulfilled.[48] If so, what does it mean to be individualized in Tillich's theology? Tillich thinks that all kind of living things have an instinct to be oneself. This process to be oneself through one's life is called individualization, but Tillich suggests that only human beings can be fully individualized. In order to explain the driving force of individuation which is called the centered self, Tillich describes it as follows:

> The term "centeredness" is derived from the geometrical circle and metaphorically applied to the structure of a being in which an effect

exercised on one part has consequence for all other parts, directly or indirectly...For where there is center, there is a periphery which includes an amount of space or, in non-metaphorical terms, which unites a manifoldness of elements.[49]

In this sense, Tillich believes that "the most individualized being is the most unapproachable and the most lonely one."[50] It implies that the most individualized people in terms of the centered self live in a morally different dimension of life, which can hardly be grasped by ordinary people. But, simultaneously, the driving force of the centered self has the greatest potentiality of participation, because each individual participates in their own world. Individuals are supposed to participate in the world because they are a part of the world. Tillich indicates that to be real human beings, we are asked to participate in the world. He believes that without participation in the world, the individual cannot exist. To experience the genuine meaning of human beings, we have to be communal beings who are intimately associated with the world. The tendency to be a person cannot be actualized solely through its potential spirit without any human community. No individual lives without participation, and no personal being survives without communal being. The communion of personal encounter provides persons with growth. As we realize our reality through encounters with others whether they accept or reject us, we can get the meaning of our being through participation in the world. We cannot expect a fully developed self without participation in other fully developed selves. Individuals can grow through participation in the world. In this sense, he insists that participation is not optional to human beings but essential. Thus, the self has been formulated and influenced through the interaction between the community and the personal. In this process, however, interaction can result in integration and disintegration. Life cannot avoid this category. Through this process the personal has chances to increase one's capacity. But, simultaneously, the personal contains a danger of disruption.[51]

Tillich's explanation about self-disintegration which is caused by two reasons implies how the self at mid-life cannot be experienced as a whole but a dispersed self which appears as stagnation at mid-life. Taking all possible content from experience, the centered self has to be confronted with a crisis, which means each of different proclivities tend to dominate the center of the personal.

Tillich shows that humans have unlimited possibilities through participation. But he believes that in spite of the fact that human beings pursue these possibilities, the possibilities are easily conquered by humans' incessant conquering desire. This is the limitation of human possibility. Actuality of human participation is different from potential participation in which human beings consider that there are no limits for participation. The more individuals are individualized, the more they can participate. Individuals participate in the world through their perception, imagination and action. But participation in the world causes the structure of destruction and all levels of evil in history.[52] In other words, the ambiguity of self-integration means a unilateral relationship, which is lopsided in the process of individuation, between the subject and the object. This lopsided process cannot invoke the movement of *eros*, because this unilateral relation means that there is no interaction between the subject and the object. In this relationship people are considered an object among objects. In this sense we all are considered to be tools among tools. Tillich points out that this is the phenomenon of estrangement. Furthermore he mentions that it causes the "structurer of self-destruction, basic sources of evil."[53]

Tillich thinks that this self-integration has been shown and experienced as morality through human history. Morality is the privilege of human beings. No other creatures can institute morality.[54] But, in spite of this privilege, morality cannot solve human's ontological problems and anxiety, because we have experienced that this morality has been replaced by "totalitarian rulers" throughout humanities tragic history. In this perspective, in Tillich's theological conception, self-integrative activities cannot overcome "totalitarian rulers" in humanity. Based on these limitations, Tillich suggests that the personal needs something which transcends and transforms us. This transcendent reality is "the Spiritual Presence/God."[55] In pointing out the limitedness of human potentiality, the self-creativity, Tillich suggests that the only way to reunite human essence and existence is the divine Spirit. The reason it can overcome or reunite the gap is due to its new reality, transcendental power

The Self-Creativity and Its Ambiguity: Dynamics and Form

The second peculiarity of the self, comparing it with other creatures, is the self-creativity which consists of *dynamics* and *form*.[56] Tillich believes that all beings have forms because they have meaning. Beings need a form. Thus without forms we cannot expect a definite being. In this sense all existing beings have their own forms. And every form has something in the form. If so what is in a form? Tillichpoints out that the something means "dynamics." Thus, Tillich points out the correlation of it as follows: "Whatever loses its form loses its being."[57] Also as he explains the meaning of dynamics he compares it with "will" (Schopenhauer), "will to power"(Nietzsche), "unconsciousness"(Freud and Hartmann), and "strife"(Jung and Scheler).[58] This ontological polarity of dynamics and form occurs in a practical life as a function of the self through the polar pattern of vitality and intentionality. In other words, we can say that the self has two functions which can be expressed internally as intentionality and externally as vitality. Vitality can be compared with dynamics, and intentionality can be compared with form. Vitality is the creative drive which seeks for new forms. Vitality and intentionality have also an inseparable connection to human beings.

> Vitality, in the full sense of the word, is human because man has intentionality. The dynamic element in man is open in all directions; it is bound by no a priori limiting structure. Man is able to create a world beyond the given world; he creates the technical and the spiritual realms....Dynamics reaches out beyond nature only in man. This is this vitality, and therefore man alone has vitality in the full sense of the world.[59]

Through the interaction between dynamics and form or vitality and intentionality human beings can create beyond limiting structures. Humanity does not stop developing its circumstances for living. Tillich calls this accumulation of self-creativity as "culture." But, in defining self-creativity, he points out that the ground of human dynamics roots itself in divine creativity. Based on this prerequisite element, life can create itself.[60]

We need to pay attention Tillich's definition of self-creativity. He suggests that self-creativity originally belongs to divine creativity. In terms of Tillich's definition of self-creativity, we know that its root is deeply related to the divine creativity which causes human beings to have this trend.

Self-creativity drives life in terms of the dynamic impulse to move from a centered self to another center, whereas self-integration forms the personal in its centeredness. Self-creativity has a centrifugal force, and self-integration has a centripetal force. But Tillich indicates the weak point of self-creativity. As life approaches death, the self-creativity confronts self-destruction. There is a life to live in the moment of conception, but, simultaneously, death waits for us. Tillich compares this destiny with the ambiguities of "life instinct" and "death instinct."[61]

In all life processes, ambiguities of self-creation and self-destruction are a basic experience of all life. Self-destruction expands not only to individuals but to all realms of creatures as well. Tillich calls this experience "a life-death-struggle," which is going on in all of "nature."[62] Not only this destiny of all living things, but also the reality of struggle is a destructive means for the self-creation of life. The creation of culture, self, and so on comes from destruction, such as war, and conflicts with other life. Tillich points out that human creativity co-exists with human atrocity, despair, and tragedy.

There are two things given to human beings from the beginning of humanity: language and technology. And these two things belong to the category of self-creativity/culture. By using human language, the personal can have an individual world. In other words, language has a power which can construct each one's world under the dimension of spirit. Humans can build up their world in order to understand themselves, but in terms of this they cannot understand the whole world. In this perspective, within the conditions of human existence, there exists a cleavage between subject and object. The personal tries to overcome or bridge the split, in terms of words, concepts, and images, between subject and object. But it never fully attains this goal. "All ambiguities of the self-creation of life" is how Tillich refers to this.[63] Language and technology are the fruit of human reason. The development of human culture has been based on this reason. And the result of accumulated reason throughout human history is technology in contemporary culture. Although technology brings us plenty of benefits, Tillich criticizes the shadow side of it. To understand Tillich's criticism, first of all, I analyze the definition of reason in Tillich's theology. By this analysis, we can figure out the power of reason and its weakness which shapes humanity. Especially, I intend to find out how these reason-based technological tendencies in our culture have influenced the self.

Regarding technology accumulated by reason, Tillich indicates three ambiguities. *1) The ambiguity of freedom and limitation in technical production.* This is expressed not only in myths and legends, but also in technical production throughout all periods. The personal wants to be united under a symbol, such as the Tower of Babel in myths, and technological productions in modernity. The result of both can be creative and destructive. *2) The ambiguity of means and ends.* In a dynamic-economic world, so long as a new need is ceaselessly engendered and satisfied, technical possibility becomes both an individual and social temptation. The production of means becomes manifest as an end in itself. *3) The ambiguity of self and thing.* In our technological world, humanity transforms all natural objects into 'things.' In this process, not only natural objects, but also humanity becomes a thing among things, which cannot be communicated. This tendency becomes so natural that natural primitivism is considered as unnatural. There are psychological sufferings in detail when people are treated as things.[64] The vitality and intentionality of the self are under the control of *hubris* and *concupiscence* which do not have a form. In this process the aim of the self is only *dynamics/vitality*. Vitality without a form means that dynamics seeks only "temptation for the new" in which distorted creativity replaces the creativity for the new. This situation results in emptiness and chaos of meaning in the self because the self is separated from a form. Also, vitality which reduces the self to a system of logical, moral, and aesthetic forms shows humanity in estrangement. Tillich believes that both types which lack the interaction show us humanity's existential predicament.[65] In this perspective what Tillich concludes from the ambiguities of self-creativity is that 'the Kingdom of God' is an inevitable answer for the ambiguities.[66]

The Self-Transcendence and Its Ambiguity: Freedom and Destiny

Self-transcendence has a polarity: *freedom* and *destiny*.[67] Tillich mentions that things do not have freedom, only human beings have freedom, because things are determined by objects which lack freedom. Freedom is the function of a human who is a rational person and a complete self. This complete self or the rational person means that all parts and functions of human beings, which constitute human beings, participate in this freedom. Because of this freedom which is the root of self-transcendence of the centered self, life wants to escape from the bondage of finitude.

> Life, in degree, is free from itself, from a total bondage to its own finitude. It is striving in the vertical direction toward ultimate and infinite being. The vertical transcends both the circular line of centeredness and the horizontal line of growth.[68]

According to Tillich this freedom is experienced through three functions: deliberation in which people express themselves through arguments and decisions in which human beings cut or exclude possibilities, and responsibility in which people have freedom to respond if they are asked about their decisions. Through these characteristics we are convinced that human freedom is not determined by any outside element of the human self but by our whole centered self.[69] Thus we have the responsible self as the result of freedom. In this vein, we can understand succinctly the meaning of human destiny in association with the meaning of freedom. In other words, the concept of freedom in human beings cannot be understood separately from destiny. Tillich points out that this inter-relationship is the basis for human centered selfhood.[70]

> When I make a decision, it is the concrete totality of everything that constitutes my being which decides, not an epistemological subject. This refers to body structure, psychic striving, spiritual character....Destiny is not a strange power which determines what shall happen to me. It is myself as given, formed by nature, history, and myself. My destiny is the basis of my freedom; my freedom participates in shaping my destiny.[71]

Through an inseparable relation between freedom and destiny Tillich articulates that the self is encompassed by destiny. Destiny is the milieu of the self. But destiny does not mean the opposite of freedom. Rather destiny forms the limits and conditions of the self. Within a person, the whole universe is the potential content of his/her centered self. The personal does not realize human destiny but thinks about infinite human freedom. But humanity's finitude is the actual limit to embrace the content of the universe. Even though human beings have some limitation, they want to take all content. Willful acts which are filled with freedom are going to fail because of human *hubris* and *concupiscence*.[72] In this sense, Tillich basically points out human deterioration from its essence. Because of this tendency human beings regard themselves as having incessant freedom through which they consider themselves the center of the universe. Tillich calls it the profanization of the self.

There is always the profanation of life in every act of the self-transcendence of life. The profanization of life has received the glory of holiness. The profane makes every subject as object, thing. Objectification is the destiny of self-transcendence. He argues that if human beings are not challenged or controlled by human destiny we shall lose the core. And then the destiny of human beings will be disregarded and unnoticed. Tillich says that human beings have lost genuine freedom because we do not understand it in terms of human destiny. That is human destiny.[73] Human meaninglessness, emptiness of living, and restlessness of life, expressed through existentialism and depth psychology, are the results of disregarding our destiny.[74] Through the Spirit one is able to sublimate human greatness. By the spirit, human greatness reveals its reliance on the ultimate Being.[75] This relation is directly connected with the quest for unambiguous life in religion. Yet, problems arise from religion, because religion occurs in the changing forms of human culture and morality. In this perspective, no religion is revealed, as it is the creation and the distortion of revelation.[76] But even though Tillich has some negative points regarding religion, he believes that religion is the answer for the unambiguous life. So to speak, religion is not the perfect answer, but the best one.

In conclusion I have researched the ambiguities of the self and its polarities in Tillich's theology to analyze and to criticize the self. Tillich shows the ontological polarities between the self and the world through three categories. He articulates that human positive potentialities need to be understood in terms of polarities which indicate human limitations. Without acknowledging these three tensions between the self and the world it is hard to understand the self in the world. His understanding of the self in terms of the polarities provides us plenty of implications for understanding the self. Although we experience the ambiguities of the centered self because of self-estrangement, Tillich's theological interpretation of the centered self reveals what are the potentialities of the centered self. And he explains human predicaments as the self-estrangement from the centered self, such as estrangement from oneself, others, and God.[77] In this sense, a given question in this situation is how the self at mid-life can be fully realized to experience the potentiality of the centered self.

Theological Direction for Renewing the Centered Self at Mid-life

The Divine Spirit and Its Influence to the Self

As indicated in the previous pages, I have reviewed the potentiality and limitedness of the centered self through self-integration (morality), self-creativity (culture), and self-transcendence (religion). In mentioning these peculiarities of the centered self Tillich suggests that these potentialities of the centered self can be reunited only by something which transcends each of them. He calls this something as "the new reality of the divine Spirit."[78]

As the personal confronts human limitedness, we move toward the ontological question: "What is being itself?"[79] This question, filled with ontological questions and existential anxieties, brings forth the shock of nonbeing as "metaphysical shock"; because of this the personal tries to transcend one's estrangement and reunite with one's essential being. But in the process they realize the impossibility of reuniting one's essential being. So, from this point, the quest for the Spiritual Presence is raised. Tillich is assured that "the Spiritual Presence" is the most important mediator which can provide people with the meaning of life.

> ...spirit as a dimension of life unites the power of being with the meaning of being. Spirit can be defined as the actualization of power and meaning in unity... This immediate experience makes it possible to speak symbolically of God as Spirit and of the divine Spirit...Without this experience of spirit as the unity of power and meaning in himself, man would not have been able to express the revelatory of "God present" in the term "Spirit" or "Spiritual Presence."[80]

From the above paragraph we need to listen carefully about the influence of the Spiritual Presence to humans. Tillich states that the Spiritual Presence has a power which can unite the split and also brings meaning for humans' life. In other words, as Tillich indicates about the ambiguities of the self and the limitations of reason, the encountering of the Spiritual Presence can result in unity and meaning for humans. But the problem of "Spiritual Presence" emerges when we enunciate it. God must transcend all the scopes of finitude to be the answer to the questions raised in the finite. Simultaneously, transcendence means loss of the concreteness of a being-to-being relation. This is the inevitable tension in the idea of God. Wherever there is the experience of God from the primitive world to the contemporary world, the conflict between concreteness and transcendence is actual.[81] This tension is the problem in defining what is the Spiritual Presence. But even though we have such difficulty in defining who/what is God, Tillich suggests that God is the answer for all questions of the finitude.[82]

The Spiritual Presence can make us bridge the gap between essence and existence through faith and love. When the Spiritual Presence grasps the personal, there will be a moment which is called "transcendent union." This transcendent union appears as the ecstatic movement in the human spirit. And the ecstatic movement from one point is called 'faith,' from another, 'love.' But these two elements are inseparable in the transcendent union.[83] Faith is not an act of cognition, neither is it subject to verification by experiment. Faith is the Spiritual Presence's action toward human's ambiguous life.[84] As Tillich observed, by this action, we are opened by the Spiritual Presence to the transcendent unity of an unambiguous life.[85] In this faith, we experience three elements: the first element is faith which is being opened by the Spiritual Presence; the second is courageous faith, which stands in the Spiritual Presence in spite of the infinite gap between the human spirit and the Spiritual Presence; the third is faith as anticipatory, expecting the continuing participation in the transcendental life. And then what does "love" mean in Tillich's theology? Tillich establishes the difference between love and faith in the following way.

> Whereas faith is the stage of being grasped by the Spiritual Presence, love is the stage of being taken by the Spiritual Presence into the transcendent unity of unambiguous life.[86]

Love is another element caused by the Spiritual Presence. Generally, according to Tillich, love implicates emotional elements and is explicit in every function of the mind. In this perspective, love is rooted in the innermost side of life itself. Love has a universal essential attribute which unites and reunites the separated. This ontological and universal particularity is effective in the following three life processes: "it unites in a center, it creates the new, and it drives beyond everything given to its ground and aim."[87] As Tillich indicates, there should be a movement from the center toward participation and a returning process, self-integration in all dimensions of life. The real participation means to acknowledge the other as a person. But in actual life this love as the basis for the intrinsic moral imperative brings ambiguity with it, because love (agape) cannot be created by the spirit of the human. Tillich says that the clue for solving this ambiguity is the creation of agape by the Spiritual Presence.[88]

As described above, love and faith have individualistic characteristics, but both are connected within an inseparable relationship. As it were, love as agape is only possible in the relation with faith. In other words, faith which involves openness, courage and anticipation toward God is only possible through the encounter with the Spiritual Presence. And love is the result of encountering the Spiritual Presence. In comparing with psychological perspectives on generativity and theological interpretations of love, generally we may not find out the difference between those. But Tillich's theological perspective on love succinctly points out that without the experience of the Spiritual Presence it is hard to bear 'love.' Consequently, the Spiritual Presence creates the New Being above the ambiguity of life.[89] But before we experience the New Being, we need to know what is the spirit in humans, because without knowing the spirit in humans, we cannot understand the Spirit.[90]

What does the spirit in human beings mean in Tillich's theology? Theological interpretations of it imply that there is a spirit given by God in the human mind. In a word, it means the image of God in humanity. The understanding of the spirit in humanity means to understand humanity based on acknowledging and accepting God's presence, the vertical commitment. Psychologically speaking, it implies human potentialities which have been described as the archetypal image of God. Tillich, mentioning overall of these functions, says that the hemisphere of human spirit is human reason. In this sense, Tillich does not deny the importance of human reason. But the problem is that as I indicated in previous chapters, it is impossible to solve human ontological and existential problems in terms of only reason. Thus, knowing the spirit in the human is a precondition to understanding what the Spirit is. What Tillich believes is that the divine Spirit works and dwells in the human spirit. It does not mean that the divine Spirit just stays human, but that it steers the human spirit out of the self.[91]

When the divine Spirit breaks into the spirit in the self, some special moment occurs, which is called "ecstasy." This ecstasy, without destroying the self, drives the spirit of the human beyond reason. This ecstasy does not destroy the centeredness of the self. Instead of destroying the self, it provides people with something that the human spirit cannot do.

> The Spiritual Presence creates an ecstasy in both of them which drives the spirit of man beyond itself without destroying its essential, i.e., rational, structure. Ecstasy does not destroy the centeredness of the integrated self...Although the ecstatic character of the experience of Spiritual Presence does not destroy the rational structure of the human spirit it does something the human spirit could not do by itself. When it grasps man, it creates unambiguous life.[92]

As Tillich researched about the ambiguities of life, humans, in their self-transcendence, seek the unambiguous life. This desire cannot become truth until humans are grasped by the Spiritual Presence.[93] The Spiritual Presence has a special purpose for finite human beings. When humans are grasped by it, they experience the meaning of self, because it has a meaning-bearing power in an ecstatic experience. In this sense, the experience of ecstasy is related to how humans can have and bear the meaning of their lives. The Spiritual Presence is absolutely necessary for a meaningful life. The meaning-bearing power of the Divine Being implies plenty of meaning for mid-lifers. As I indicated, the problems of mid-life, such as meaninglessness and ontological anxieties in terms of the fear of death/non-being and human contextual problems, can be solved and integrated by encountering the Spiritual Presence. In this aspect, it is crucial to overcome the anxieties and crisis of male mid-lifers in terms of experiencing the Spiritual Presence. As Tillich indicates, encountering the Spiritual Presence does not mean to disregard the presence of human living, but it can make us see beyond human reason. Tillich's theological understanding of the Spiritual Presence tells us how much the encountering of the Spiritual Presence is crucial to the life cycle in the second half of life, which is supposed to live based on spiritual perspectives.

Theological Understandings of New Being as the Recovering the Centered Self

Tillich's concept of "New Being" has plenty of similarity to the concept of "generativity." But, theologically speaking there is a difference between "new being" and "generativity". Whereas "generativity" as human instinct in Erikson's psychosocial theory is based on one's mature psychological developmental stages, the possibility of "new being" is rooted in encountering the Spiritual Presence. The Spiritual Presence, creating the New Being who overcomes the ambiguity of life through the two characters, love and faith, generates the transcendent unity of unambiguous life. Tillich thinks that when the Spiritual Presence is experienced in a personal life, it makes an unambiguous life. This unambiguous life is not perfect. But the unambiguous life means a different quality from the ambiguous life; it is a fragmental, partial, and unfulfilled process. Although this experience is partial and unfulfilled, it shows some possibility of essential unity with God. Tillich describes this as follows:

> This distinction between the ambiguous and the fragmentary makes it possible for us to full affirmation and full commitment to the manifestations of the Spiritual Presence while remaining aware of the fact that in the very acts of affirmation and commitment the ambiguity of life reappears. Awareness of this situation is the decisive criterion for religious maturity. It belongs to the quality of the New Being that it puts its own actualization in time and space under the criteria by which it judges the ambiguities of life in general. Yet in doing so, the New Being does conquer(though fragmentarily) the ambiguities of life in time and space.[94]

One's being in confronting the threat of death, and the anxiety of the future and past causes us to be in fear.[95] The fear of the past which has disappeared in the running of time, and the future which has not certainly appeared to us, forces people to fall into a state of anxiety based ontological questions and anxiety. This threat "is conquered by the freedom of God toward the past and its potentialities. The anxiety of the future is conquered by the dependence of the new on the unity of the divine life."[96] Tillich points out the limits of the self in terms of time and space. But Tillich argues that humans can overcome the limitations of the self through the Spiritual Presence. Even though this experience cannot be a perfect one it can partially overcome the limitation of the self. The Spiritual Presence as God who is eternal is the basis for humanity's courage to participate in time. These sorts of participation, such as time and a desire to be transformed to the New Being, however, are a vague dream until we have the experience of transcendental union with the Spiritual Presence even though the desire to be the New Being is a universal quest.[97]

Tillich argues that to be the New Being universally is based on human ambiguity. In other words, because of the universal ambiguities of human beings, the expectation of the New Being is universal. Theologically speaking, wanting to be generative persons or New Beings reveals that we have not realized the archetypal image of God. In this sense such tendencies of human desires imply human ambiguities, because if we experience the new being or the archetypal image of God, we do not ask the new being. In this sense, Tillich emphasizes that to be New Being is absolutely necessary prior to new acting. In other words, bad trees cannot bear good fruits, but good trees bear good fruits. Tillich's emphasis on the New Being before new acting points out critically the weakness of psychological understanding of male mid-lifer tendencies such as generativity of Erik H. Erikson and the archetypal image of God of Carl G. Jung. Of course, Tillich partially accepts that generative tendencies and human potentialities through the archetypal image of God are associated with the unambiguous and ultimate.[98] But these psychological interpretations emphasize only human potentialities and its human psychological developmental fruits. Tillich articulates that all human endeavors which try to overcome human existential estrangement have failed and the endeavors have brought forth toil and tragic failures which we have experienced through human history. Thus, Tillich defines that human beings are in bondage to human evil will.[99]

We all have such a desire to overcome human bondages which bind us to selfish desires which have destroyed oneself, one's neighbors and global community. Tillich suggests that the misery of humanity cannot be changed, but in terms of personal experiences with the Spiritual Presence each individual can transcend one's given milieu and ambiguities. It means that transformed individuals can have a transformed quality which can affect the social milieu. In this sense Tillich emphasizes that transformed reality of individuals is expected to participate in a horizontal transforming process based on one's vertical dimension with the Spiritual Presence. The essential purpose of becoming the New Being is the expectation of a transformed reality.[100] So, experiencing the New Being is considered the ultimate concern for human beings. And this desire of New Being is not optional but we all are asked to participate in the process of New Being.[101]

The reason humans are eager to be transformed is that humans have realized some inevitable limitedness of the finite, which is the gap between the essential and the existential. In the essential, it may be like the confession of St. Paul:

> I do not do what I want, but I do the very thing I hate... For I know that nothing good dwells within me, that is, in my flesh. I can will what is right, but I cannot do it... Wretched man that I am! Who will rescue me from this body of death?"(NRSV, Romans 7).

If we experience the Spiritual Presence, it can be replaced by a "before" and "after." The creative ground does not manifest itself, however, until humans reunite with the Spiritual Presence. Here we need to pay attention to the role of the Spiritual Presence. Tillich definitely argues that we may not experience the creative ground, which I want to compare with the archetypal image of God, until we reunite with the Spiritual Presence.[102]

The very initiative of reunion with the Spiritual Presence is called "conversion." According to Tillich, this conversion experience brings a meaning-bearing power for human life through an ecstatic experience.[103] But it cannot be explained by a particular moment, because it should be a continuing process throughout one's life. The experience of "new being" can be experienced through encountering the Spiritual Presence in terms of conversion experiences which acknowledge one's ambiguities and limitations. As seen in the previous paragraph, the encounter with the Spiritual Presence brings us to stages. And the first stage of encountering the Spiritual Presence is regeneration which is called a conversion experience. Tillich defines conversion as:

> Conversion can have the character of a transition from the latent stage of the Spiritual Community to its manifest stage. This is the real structure of conversion; it implies that repentance is not completely new and that neither is faith... There is no absolute conversion, but there is relative conversion before and after the central event of somebody's "repenting" and "believing," of somebody's being grasped by the Spiritual Presence in a fertile moment, a Kairos.[104]

Individuals experience the conversion moment, the fertile moment, Kairos, as the healing process occurs within individuals. Tillich refers to "Spiritual personalities" as those whom experience the Spiritual Presence. He expresses this healing as salvation. The result of encountering the Spiritual Presence means to become a "New Being." The result of "New Being" can be divided into three categories: creativity, regeneration, and eschatology.[105] In terms of these categories "new being" can destroy unbelief, hubris, and concupiscence.[106] These three categories can be associated with the concept of generativity in psychosocial theory. Those who are in this stage have a desire to be creative. And their goals and life are based on the experience of regeneration which can make them open up to the meaning of a spiritual life, the second half of life.

"New Being" does not mean merely difference from "old being." As Tillich points out, experiencing "new being" means to experience "spiritual personality," which implies renewal from old being. Old being implies corruption, distortion, and split, which have been destroyed. In mentioning about old being, Tillich points out that it is not completely destroyed but almost destroyed. But in terms of encountering the Spiritual Presence, old beings experience a *re*-newal: *re*-conciliation, *re*-union, and *re*-surrection.[107] These categories show that the Spiritual Presence does not create new elements in human beings but recreate and renew what has been neglected and repressed of the image of God. But the archetypal image of God cannot be completed through human endeavors because human beings bring their own self limitations as Tillich points out in previous chapters.

The term "renew" means to revive the estranged character under existential being. Also this renewal implies a transformation from existential beings estranged to essential beings that reveal potential character.[108] So *re*-newal means first to rebuild the destroyed and hidden image of God within oneself in terms of the Spiritual Presence, and then it makes us open toward others and God. Tillich argues that the peculiar characteristic of old being is the separation of people from people. The reason people estrange oneself from others is rooted in people's estrangement from themselves. In other words, estrangement implies three categories: oneself, others, and God. And also renewal means with oneself, others, and God.[109] In this respect, in Tillich's theology, "New Being" implies healing which means to be reunited from estrangement, given a center from splitting, between oneself ,others, and God.

Theological Implication of Healing for Male Mid-life Crisis

It is inevitable to talk about "new being" as healing associated with salvation in Tillich's theology. Also this concept of healing needs to be understood in connection with the concept of salvation. Tillich defines salvation as transferring into the New Being.[110] This salvation, which transcends the structure of the finite being, is uncovered only in Spiritual Presence. This moment called revelation or ecstatic reason, which can happen through the encountering with the Spiritual Presence, provides people with the presence of God. God is the ground of being, who is also the ground of the ontological structure. God participates in this ontological structure, but also transcends this structure. God's participation in the finite brings out the manifestation of shaking, transforming, and healing power.[111] In this sense Tillich articulates that where there is new being there will be new creation. And this new creation implies salvation. The most meaningful purpose of salvation is to find out one's ultimate meaning for existence. In this perspective, Tillich states that the purpose of pastoral care or counseling is to invite people to the ultimate concern.[112] To "prevent the self-destructive structure of existence from plunging mankind into complete annihilation" is what Tillich states as the purpose of healing.[113] Tillich's definition of salvation is very close to the meaning of healing in psychology. He articulates that the general understanding of salvation means to be saved from ultimate negative meanings of life. The negative meaning of life is divided into four categories in Tillich's theology. First, he insists that the ultimate negative of life is the eternal death. Through psychological research I argue that one of the main causes of male mid-life crisis comes from the fear of death, from desiring immortality. In the same vein, Tillich argues that the fear of death makes us have negative living patterns. The power of death is influential to human behaviors. It makes all of us fall into despair. Secondly, those who do not have the inner purpose (*telos*) of life are in ultimate despair. Tillich does not mention the external goal of life. Salvation means to grasp the real meaning of one's life. In this sense, Tillich talks about the inner *telos* of life. Thirdly, if we do not have any unity with the Kingdom of God, it implies that we are in ultimate despair. Lastly, salvation means to be saved from the exclusion from eternal life.[114] Thus, in these definitions of salvation, Tillich points out that where there is the healing power as salvation there will be prevention of self-destruction and annihilation.

> ...healing means reuniting that which is estranged, giving a center to what is split, overcoming the split between God and man, man and his world, man and himself. Out of this interpretation of salvation, the concept of the New Being has grown.[115]

In terms of preventing self-destruction and annihilation through encountering the Spiritual Presence, which is called revelation in Tillich's theology, people can get a centering power which renews our distorted image of God. What is important from this renewal is that there are three parts which need to be reconciled: God and individual, individual and one's world, and oneself. Through reconciliation with God, others, and oneself by encountering the Spiritual Presence people can be transformed from their ultimate negativity to ultimate positivity. So those who are reconciled can have influence to transform individuals and community.

Tillich explains in detail the function of the Spiritual Presence as it encounters people. As we encounter the Spiritual Presence, it ceaselessly challenges us to recognize that our life is aimless, empty and meaningless. This Spirit awakens us to have desire to strive for the sublimation of the profanity of daily life. Also it gives us positive courage even though we have experienced destructiveness around us. The Spirit can give courage to us to be reconciled with people whom we have hurt deeply, and provide us with love for those whom we dislike and hate. Furthermore, the Spiritual Presence can annihilate our sloth for the *telos* of our life and transform depression and aggression to stability.[116]

In conclusion, Tillich defines salvation as healing which is based on the inner meaning of life. What he believes is that this inner meaning by the Spirit can transform not only oneself but also others. But what is important is that as human history has ambiguities, the experience of new being also has ambiguities. In other words, the experience of New Being can be experienced through encountering the Spiritual Presence. But this experience is the first stage to the New Being. It takes a process. The experience of the Spiritual Presence means "already" but the result of it means "not yet." It takes a life term process.[117] This process is not a momentary one, but a continuous process, and also implies fragmentary elements to humans.

Summary

Tillich heavily emphasizes the limitation of the self. First of all, before analyzing the tendencies of the self, he suggests that the self is estranged from the ground of being. In describing the tendencies of the self he insists three self-centeredness tendencies: unbelief, hubris, and concupiscence. And he believes that all these tendencies are universal.[118] He thinks that "unbelief" is the representative characteristic of human personality. Humanity does not want to place God as the center of themselves. "Hubris" indicates human total self-elevation/inflated self. In terms of this tendency we feel human greatness and dignity and transcend oneself and the world, but it is also temptation; we are tempted to take a role as the center of universe. So the self does not accept its finitude and endows itself with infinite attributes. The last one is "concupiscence." Tillich does not only categorize it into a specific area, such as sexual desire, but also to other areas such as physical hunger, knowledge, material wealth and spiritual values. But to fulfil these desires the self has to conquer and destroy others. And this tendency appears in existential literature, psychology, philosophy and art. But according to Tillich what is more important than this phenomenon is that all these desires of the self are deeply connected with the desire of the self to reunite with the whole, God. Because we are existentially estranged from the whole, in spite of our ontological rootedness in God, we thirst to experience it.

Tillich analyzes ontological polarities of the self: self-integration(morality), self-creativity(culture) and the self-transcendence(religion). In realization of the self, self-integration is inevitable. But to experience self-realization the self or individual has to participate in the world, because without participation in it, self-realization does not have any meaning. But through interaction individuals experience integration and disintegration. For this reason the self experiences a danger of disruption. As a result, individuals through participation are regarded as tools among tools. It causes "structure of self-destruction, basic sources of evil."[119] Self-creativity has a polarity of *dynamic* and *form*. Dynamics implies the vitality of the self and form has the intentionality of the self. In terms of dynamics or vitality the humans can create a world, including the technical and the spiritual realms, which is beyond human limitation. In other words, the vitality of humanity can make a world beyond nature. But in this process, because of human self-centeredness which tends to go beyond a given world, human vitality loses a form, a given world, which brings out the emptiness and chaos of meaning of the self. And self-creativity confronts self-destruction. Self-transcendence has a polarity of *freedom* and *destiny*. Human beings have freedom to choose all things for themselves. In this sense, the human self does not realize its limits but wants its infinity. Through this the human self considers itself as the center of the universe which results in the profanization of the self throughout human history. So Tillich believes that this self-elevation or inflated self tendency should be challenged by human destiny. All these three polarities of the self reveal the peculiarities of the self in a macrocosmic and microcosmic perspective. In the same vein Tillich affirms that all these polarities also reveal that the self is rooted in the divine self. For this reason, although the self experiences the limitation of it, it tries to go beyond its category. This desire is regarded as universal in Tillich's theology. Tillich suggests the Divine Spirit can recreate and renew the centered self without destroying the structure of the self. The encounter with the Divine Spirit brings shaking, transforming, and healing power to people through renewing the neglected and oppressed image of God. In this sense, Tillich mentions that the purpose of pastoral counseling is to invite people to the "ultimate concern" through which they are protected from self-destruction and experience the re-centered self.

(Notes)

1. Paul Tillich, *Systematic Theology*, Vol. 1 (Chicago: The University of Chicago Press, 1951), 60, Hereafter abbreviated as *ST*.
2. Ibid., 8.
3. Ibid., 22.
4. Paul Tillich, *The Meaning of Health: Essays in Existentialism, Psychoanalysis and Religion,* ed. Perry LeFevre, (Chicago: Exploration Press at The Chicago Theological Seminary, 1984), 88.
5. *ST*. Vol. 1, 169.
6. *ST*. Vol. 2, 49.
7. Ibid., 45-49.
8. Ibid.
9. Ibid.
10. Ibid., 44-47.
11. Ibid., 59.
12. Ibid., 47.
13. Ibid., 45.
14. Ibid., 47-52.
15. Ibid
16. Ibid., 48.
17. Ibid.
18. Ibid., 47.
19. Ibid.
20. Ibid., 49.

21. Ibid.
22. Ibid., 50.
23. Ibid., 51.
24. Ibid., 51-52.
25. Ibid., 52.
26. Ibid.
27. Ibid., 54.
28. Ibid.
29. Ibid., 55.
30. Ibid., 52-53.
31. Edward F. Edinger, *Ego and Archetype: Individuation and the Religious Function of the Psyche* (Boston & London: Shambhala, 1992), 3.
32. *ST.* Vol. 2, 52.
33. Ibid., 60.
34. Ibid.
35. Ibid.
36. Ibid., 61.
37. Ibid.
38. Ibid., 62.
39. Ibid., 61.
40. Ibid., 62.
41. *ST.* Vol. 3, 30.
42. *ST.* Vol. 1, 169.
43. *ST.* Vol. 3, 30.
44. Ibid., 32.
45. Ibid., 30.
46. Ibid., 31.
47. Ibid.
48. Ibid., 32.
49. Ibid., 32-33.
50. Ibid., 33.
51. Ibid., 33-34.
52. *ST.* Vol. 2, 66.
53. Ibid.
54. *ST.* Vol. 3, 38.
55. Ibid., 44.
56. Ibid., 50-57.
57. *ST.* Vol. 1, 178.
58. Ibid., 179.
59. Ibid., 180.
60. *ST.* Vol. 3., 50.
61. Ibid., 56.
62. Ibid., 53.
63. Ibid., 72.
64. Ibid., 92.
65. *ST.* Vol. 2, 65.

66. *ST.* Vol. 3, 74.
67. Ibid., 86-88.
68. Ibid., 86-87.
69. *ST.* Vol. 1, 183-84.
70. Ibid.,184.
71. Ibid.,185
72. *ST.* Vol. 2, 62.
73. Ibid., 63.
74. Ibid.
75. Ibid.
76. Ibid.
77. Ibid., 44.
78. *ST.* Vol. 3, 44.
79. *ST*, Vol. 2, 186.
80. *ST.* Vol. 3, 111.
81. *ST.* Vol. 1, 211.
82. Ibid.
83. *ST.* Vol. 3, 129.
84. Ibid., 133.
85. Ibid., 131.
86. Ibid., 134.
87. Ibid.
88. Ibid., 135.
89. Ibid., 138, 139.
90. Ibid., 22.
91. Ibid.,112.
92. Ibid.
93. Ibid.
94. Ibid., 140.
95. Ibid., 270.
96. Ibid., 276.
97. *ST*, Vol. 2, 86.
98. Ibid., 79.
99. Ibid., 79-80.
100. Ibid., 88.
101. Paul Tillich, *New Being* (New York: Charles Scribner's Sons, 1955), 17.
102. *ST.* Vol. 2, 226.
103. Ibid., 115.
104. *ST*, Vol. 3, 220.
105. *ST.* Vol. 1, 55.
106. *ST.* Vol. 2, 177.
107. Paul Tillich, *New Being*, 20.
108. *ST.* Vol. 2, 120.
109. Paul Tillich, *New Being*, 23.
110. *ST*, Vol. 2, 166.
111. *ST*, Vol. 3, 167.

112. Paul Tillich, "Theology and Counseling" in *The Meaning of Health*, 117.
113. *ST.* Vol. 2, 167.
114. Ibid., 165.
115. Ibid., 166.
116. Paul Tillich, *The Eternal Now*, (New York: Charles Scribner's Sons, 1963), 65.
117. Ibid., 120.
118. *ST.* Vol. 2, 50-51.
119. Ibid., 66.

PART III

Pastoral Implications and Interventions for Male Mid-life Crisis

Chapter 5

A Critical Dialogue of Psychology and Theology on Male Mid-life Crisis

As males pass through mid-life they experience various human limitations, such as death, indirectly and directly which they have never felt seriously in the first half of life. It is the first element which challenges male mid-lifers to consider the meaning of life in social milieus. As I reviewed psychologists' explanations on mid-life in Part I, Erik Erikson, Elliott Jaques, Daniel Levinson, and Don McAdams all believe that immortality is one of the essential elements which causes male mid-life crisis. Immortality means to leave values to future generations or communities and it reflects the human instinct to live forever or to be remembered eternally by people. At this point it is impossible to separate the cause of male mid-life crisis from the threat of death and human longing for immortality. These two elements are inseparable in the understanding of male mid-life.

The archetypal image of God as the self in the collective unconscious, which is deeply associated with immortality, is the second element to stimulate the human psyche at mid-life. It is a desire to understand the meaning of one's life in terms of reunion with God. In these two perspectives, I will dialogue psychologically and theologically regarding the two elements so as to bring out the framework for pastoral counseling for male mid-life crisis.

Mortality as Non-being and Immortality as Desiring to Experience the Centered Self

As males approach middle age they begin to realize that their physical strength is no longer like that of young adults or adolescents. Inexhaustible passion in youth disappears, and changes of physical functions and the experience of the death of parents, relatives, and friends becomes reality to male mid-lifers. In terms of lessening of strength people begin to acknowledge their own limitations where they once considered themselves to be infinite. In fact, most people seldom think of death until middle age. Generally, we think of death when our remaining time is shorter than our lived time. When we hear or see people die who had intimate relations with us we begin to have a deep sense of death.[1] In this period, individuals begin to think their lives in terms of "time left to live" versus "time since birth."[2] In this given limitation, the reality of coming death makes individuals accept their finitude.

In general, there are seven types of fear of death, which we expect from a general perspective: 1) Loss of ability to have experiences; 2) Loss of ability to predict subsequent events; 3) Loss of our bodies; 4) Loss of ability to care for people who are dependent on us; 5) Loss of a loving relationship with our family; 6) Loss of opportunity to compete treasured plans and projects; 7) Loss of being in a relatively painless stage.[3] These seven types of loss due to death explain psychological anxiety. Of course, the actual threat of death at mid-life is not close to mid-lifers, but we can assume substantial or potential fear of death at mid-life in terms of this explanation. And this potential fear of death at mid-life can be rightly explained in terms of the theological concept of non-being in Tillich's theology as I mentioned in chapter 4. Tillich indicates that the "shock of nonbeing" makes people raise the ontological questions of being. And he declares that "anxiety" is a result of it.[4] This anxiety is the basic quality of human beings. The anxiety is caused by realizing that we are based on nothingness. Thus, fundamentally, anxiety cannot disappear through action. Tillich mentions that the fundamental cause of human ontological anxiety comes from the fear of death, because ultimately it makes people into non-beings.[5] Among many ontological anxieties, the most serious suffering of being, in an ontological view, is losing oneself through death.[6]

Tillich thinks that everything, all categories of reality and thought, is finitude, because participation in the categories of being means to be mixed with non-being. In other words, he points out that all beings in the process of being go toward non-being.[7] The evidence which proves that we are all finite can be seen from the standpoint of potential infinity. For this reason the challenges of the infinite make us realize the limitation of the finite. As individuals confront this limitedness, they move toward the ontological question: "What is being itself?"[8] Tillich profoundly describes the anguish of being as follows:

> The question of being is produced by the "shocking of nonbeing."
> Only man can ask th e ontological question because he alone is able
> to look beyond the limits of his own being and of every other being.[9]

Tillich describes the shock of nonbeing as "metaphysical shock." This shock appeals to some deep anxiety of being: "why is there something?; why not nothing?"[10] "Nothingness" means to have limitation in comparison with the infinite. "Nothingness" causes the ontological anxiety which is clearly separated from psychological fear.[11] Tillich compares this feeling of nothingness to human beings who realize their limitations as "mortals."[12] In terms of the limitation, Tillich classifies the finite into four categories which restrict human beings as non-being; time, space, causality and substance. He thinks that in terms of the four categories human beings' identity has been grasped and shaped.[13] I will explore how Tillich's theological interpretation of the four categories of humanity can describe the human experience of death and immortality.

When can we feel that time is running? Is it possible to realize its speed in the first half of life? In the early stages of life we consider time to be unlimited, and it is even hard to think about the concept of time. But it is a different story to feel time passing and time left at mid-life. Most people hardly consider death until middle age. People gradually recognize their given time, the limitation of the finite, through experiences of mid-life. This is what Carl Jung indicates about the concept of time at mid-life. To Tillich, time is a representative category of finitude. Time, in fact, implies two meanings. One is time which we spent in the early stage of life. The other is time left to life. Both implications explain the limitation of time, because time spent is something we cannot re-collect, and time left will soon be past time. In this sense, the challenge of time is the threat of death to human beings. Death reveals the ontological character of time. We know that time is moving toward death, non-being, through which we experience the anxiety of transitoriness. Thus, the negative sense of death is the transitoriness of all things and the impossibility of holding a "present time" within the stream of time. Because of this absolute challenge of time to humankind, being toward non-being is the melancholy awareness as a theme of artistic works in all nations. So, Tillich regards that time is the essential category of finitude.[14]

The second category of finitude is space which creates the present through its union with time. Space implies two dimensions; physical space and social space. In other words, every being tries to preserve and create a space for itself, such as body, home, city, and world. And social space means groups which are focused on a structure of value and meaning. This category also implies humans' finite characteristic because without this categorical tendency it is hard to survive. As it were, space united with time implies the survival tendency of human beings. But what is important is that all spaces belong to a transitory moment. It is not permanency or eternity which can protect and sustain us from the challenge of non-being. In a historical view, there are no permanent spaces which cannot be demolished as time goes on. In a personal view, there are no eternal spaces which can stay with human beings because of the human tendency to the momentary. Because of this transitory tendency of space, Tillich compares human life with a "pilgrim on earth."[15] Pilgrim means those who consider all belongings as temporary, because visible things are not eternal things which can give real meaning to life. Being can be satisfied in terms of space temporarily. But this satisfaction cannot continue because of finitude of both sides. Losing something which beings have brings out anxiety.[16]

Ultimate insecurity happens when we do not have definite and final space, and this brings out anxiety about our human future. This is called the anxiety of existence. Such anxiety regarding an insecure future forces us to protect ourselves through creating a secure place physically and socially. Psychologically speaking, our anxiety of space, such as social and geographical anxiety, which is tightly connected with time, also points out our destiny. Whatever we have materially and mentally, such as property and joy of knowledge, cannot be ours. All of these will vanish in terms of human destiny and death. Thus, psychological anxiety at mid-life comes from a realization of human limitations, because everything that we have through material and human relations is transitory and cannot be continued eternally. As the concept of time points out human limitations, space also brings forth the vanity of all relationships. It is also the challenge of non-being to human beings.

Causality is ambiguous like time and space. Causality implies the cause and the effect of things. Causality shows a casual sequence. In this category of causality we can figure out the cause of power through which things move, and by which they are sustained. It is the positive side of causality. But there is also a negative side of causality. Finite human beings and things are not self-caused. Human beings, all things, and all creatures are thrown into being by the first cause, Being-itself. In other words, all creatures, including inanimate objects and animate objects, are not caused by themselves, because all these things do not have the power of coming into themselves. In this sense, there occurs a universal question, "Where from?"[17] Even the highest being should ask the question, "Where have I come from?"[18] Indicating this ontological question, Tillich categorizes it into a universal question which cannot be avoided by human efforts. The reason we are supposed to ask these ontological questions is that we are not beings who create ourselves and other objects. In other words, we are not absolute. We are in anxiety, because we are not absolute.[19]

In a word, causality is the question about God and human finitude; Who is God? Why does God create us? What does it mean to be human beings? What does God expect from human beings? All these questions are associated with the question of causality in Tillich's theology. Also these questions are religious questions.

Psychologically speaking about causality, all these religious ontological questions are associated with the anxiety of mid-lifers. The anxiety of mid-lifers comes from their existential struggle to figure out their cause. In this sense as indicated in previous chapters, Carl G. Jung points out that people need to live in a religious perspective in the second half of life. If we do not find religious meaning in the second half of life, we fall into stagnation. The cause of anxiety at mid-life is the longing for God. At mid-life most people ask ontological questions regarding life, death, and God. But all these questions are ontological movements to understand who we are in terms of the First cause, God.

Substance is the last category of the finite. This substance has a natural relationship with accidents. A correlational nexus exists between substance and accidents, because the substance expresses itself through the accidents. But the problem is that changing accidents threaten the substance of people or objects, which are threatened by non-being. In other words, substance is the entity which the essential core of everything. But in order to be shown, the substance has to go through the stage of accidents which can express the essential core. This process is inevitable to expressing the substance. But, in this process, changing from substance implies a lack of substantiality. The problem is that changing accidents threatens the substance of people or objects, which may be threatened by non-being. In this perspective, Tillich points out that everything finite has inherent anxiety about the loss of its substance. Also this anxiety involves the final loss of substance because of continuous change. Tillich suggests that every change which is an attribute of the finite exposes the relative non-being. From this limitation all people or objects are encompassed by anxiety and raise questions about the unchangeable.[20]

Tillich, in this final category of human finitude, points out the limitations of human beings in connection with their identity in personal and social settings. We are challenged to identify ourselves throughout our life stages in social contexts. Psychologically, one's self-identity through an interaction between oneself and one's social milieu reveals "who am I" to oneself and others. In this sense, Tillich again indicates that whatever we think and identify is partially right but not absolutely. What Tillich wants to emphasize in this category is that there is nothing eternal in the human world. Conversely, because of human finitude, human beings are unconsciously or consciously seeking eternity which can overcome the contradiction between the substance and the accidents. Psychologically speaking, this fear of defectiveness between the substance and the accidents reveals the anxiety of mid-life. Thus it is called the identity crisis at mid-life. What formulated one's identity in the first half of life cannot be considered as a permanent standard or a rule to identity - "who am I" - in the second half of life anymore.

So far I have explained the four categories of human finitude, which are theologically associated with "death", connected with the mid-life. The common result of the four categories is non-being, and this non-being brings forth anxiety,[21] because non-being for humans shakes the entire meaning of life. In this sense, non-being is a shock to human beings. This anxiety is the basic quality of human beings. Thus, anxiety cannot disappear through action. The essential quality of this anxiety comes from the insecurity of being. More concretely speaking, "nothingness" of being brings out the anxiety of being, which is inescapable to being. But Tillich distinguishes the meaning of fear and anxiety. Merely "fear," which can be conquered by action, comes from external elements such as danger, an enemy or pain. But "anxiety" comes from "inside" and "nothingness," for anxiety occurs through the structure of the finite.[22] In this sense, male mid-life crisis does not imply males' fear of death, but rather anxiety of death which can demolish what we have and what we know, which should result in the limitation of life and meaninglessness of life.

In conclusion, anxiety because of nothingness and insecurity is associated with humans' anxiety of limitations. If we were satisfied with the fate of death, we would not desire eternity. We are not satisfied with human destiny because we desire something beyond our fate. If we were satisfied with human fate, we would not feel any anxiety of nothingness. The reason we are anxious at mid-life to seek our identity is that we are beings who go beyond present beings. In this sense, I think that we are ontologically connected with God, and this indicates the archetypal image of God which I will explore in the next part. At this point, Tillich indicates that the cause of ontological anxiety is due to the destined relationship of the finite to God. Because of this people are not satisfied with the results of finitude.[23]

Through the above example of Tillich's theological understanding of human beings, we can find an interesting interpretation of Tillich; "Being-itself is not infinity; it is that which lies beyond the polarity of finitude and infinite self-transcendence." This sentence shows that human beings are associated with two categories. One is that we are finite and the other is we have infinite self-transcendence. In this sense, in the experience of the finite we call human beings the "mortals." And, in the perspective of infinite self-transcendence we name ourselves the "immortals." Tillich regards this immortality to be the divine image of human beings. In other words, the reason male mid-lifers have experienced a crisis is that as they experience the stage of mid-life they encounter so many possibilities of death they begin to acknowledge the limitations of human beings. And they recognize the destiny of human life so that based on the experience of mortality they want to be more creative and meaningful beings. Levinson points out that this tendency comes from the human desire for immortality.[24] As a way of immortality mid-lifers desire to create a legacy. And this desire to create a legacy is regarded as "altruism" for "a vehicle for the search for immortality" in Levinson's psychological analysis.[25] Furthermore Levinson indicates this desire for immortality at mid-life expresses the human desire for an "eternal soul" as an ordinary human urge.[26] Not only Levinson but also Erikson indicates that being generative is due to one's desire for immortality and is regarded as an instinctual power which can apply to all kinds of people.[27] Of course both scholars regard that for generativity or legacy we need a successful and good enough psychological development.[28] Tillich's explanation of how immortality is associated with the divine image of men is helpful for a psychological understanding of the cause of mid-life crisis.[29]

To understand more concretely the meaning of immortality and mortality, Tillich's explanation about non-being is helpful. He explains that there are two kinds of non-being. The one is *me on*, and the other is *ouk on*. *Ouk on* means "nothing" which does not have any relations with being, and *me on* also means "nothing" but it has a dialectical relationship with being. The Greeks regarded *me on* as that which does not have being, but which can become being if it is linked with ideas or essence.[30] At this point, the threat of death and non-being at mid-life does not mean *ouk on* but *me on*. Non-being as *me on* always presents dangerous and threatening situations to human beings in terms of a polar tension. For this reason, human beings always have the possibility of failing their potentialities. And there is the threat of meaninglessness of life, in addition to the threat of nothingness. But we can overcome male mid-life identity/crisis by uniting anxiety and essence. In other words, as long as we do not have any connection with Being-itself through which we can sublimate our limitedness, we may experience the chaos of individuals and communities. Thus, male mid-lifers of *me-on* are linked with God and can create and leave a legacy through our generativity because we are recovering the divine image as the centered self. Tillich's explanation of *me-on* gives us some possibilities for developing and sublimating male mid-life crisis when we relate to and approach God although we are non-beings who can easily fall in the dialectical-practical problem of stagnation at mid-life.

The Archetypal Image of God as the Centered Self

As I mentioned previously Tillich points out that the threat or anxiety of non-being is directly related to the meaninglessness of social as well as individual reality. And this kind of meaninglessness brings forth an existential despair about human destiny.[31] But because of the ontological root connected with the divine center, we can raise a question: why are human beings supposed to ask existential and essential questions based on the "ontological root?" Regarding these questions, Tillich answers that God, the origin of the finite, sustains the finite and directs it for a unity of fulfillment with God as the basic answer to the human being's situation in being.[32] Because of this tendency in human beings, seeking a unity of fulfillment with God, human beings ask the question of the "ground of being," and "eternal now."[33]

Tillich indicates that all these terms, such as "eternal now" and "ground of being," verify that human beings have ontological courage through which we may overcome the anxiety of the finite. The reason we can take this ontological courage is that human beings belong to God, but, simultaneously, we are estranged from God. In other words, existentially speaking, we are separated from God, but ontologically speaking, we are associated with God. Because of this reason, there is an inseparable relationship between God and human beings.

> Man must ask about the infinite from which he is estranged, although it belongs to him; he must ask about that which gives him the courage to take his anxiety upon himself.[34]

Tillich believes that in terms of ontological courage humans overcome meaninglessness and anxiety. Ontological courage accepts the anxiety that comes from losing one's identity and guides people to be involved in a creative life, work and love.[35] Ontological courage expresses itself in cultural creations, forms and institutions in terms of the practice of creative intentionality. But the same question is raised about this courage. How is such a courage possible? This courage is rooted in ontological courage as Tillich mentioned. In Carl Jung's perspective this courage is related to the "archetypal image of God," which cannot be erased or rooted out because of any external reasons.[36] In mentioning the psychology of Carl Jung, Tillich states that the meaning of archetype in Jung's psychology implies the ecstatic character of the unconscious.

> It is important that Jung attributes to the archetypes another ontological status than that attributed to the symbols. They are potentialities, which the symbols are actualization conditioned by the individual and social situations. The archetypes lie in the unconscious and break into the conscious life in experiences which show something of the ecstatic character attributed to revelatory experiences.[37]

What Tillich wants to emphasize in this paragraph is that the archetype does not represent the existential status of human beings but the ontological status of the centered self. The archetypal image of God is an instinct which cannot be nullified or extricated by any inner or outer causes. It is a destiny of human beings in relation to God. Because of this connection, we have courage against non-being. In other words, the reason we are challenged to realize our meaning of life in spirituality at mid-life is due to the archetypal image of God which is existentially disconnected but ontologically connected with the divine center. In order to understand the real meaning of ontological courage, Tillich defines courage. He divides the periods into three categories in order to explain it. Tillich's definition of courage through the periods can give insights into what "courage" is in a theological perspective and also a psychological perspective. The first period was the Enlightment in which people considered themselves as the bearers of reason. In other words, courage at the time meant to follow reason and to oppose irrational authority. In terms of courage based on reason, people dared to confront the destiny of human beings, death. Courage was considered as having a transforming power based on reason. In this sense, the meaning of courage in the Enlightment meant to consider oneself as a bridge toward a higher stage of rationality from a lower stage.[38] The second period is the Romantic. In this period, an individual is regarded as an infinitely significant expression of the essence of being. The individual being cannot be compared with any other thing. In this point, creative possibilities of individuals means the uniqueness of individuals. Tillich's criticism of both definitions of courage is critical. He thinks that courage defined in the Enlightment period was based on only reason which could not see the other side of it, and in the Romantic period inflated the individual beyond individuals' ability and made individuals empty.[39] The commonality between the two peculiarities of courage in each period is in the effort to evaluate self-affirmation of the self although human beings are not in non-being, fate. In other words, in terms of self-affirmation, people try to formulate a significant microcosmic universe against fate.[40]

> The courage to be as oneself in all these groups has the character of the self-affirmation of the individual self as individual self in spite of the elements of nonbeing threatening it. The anxiety of fate is conquered by the self-affirmation of the individual as an infinitely significant microcosmic representation of the universe. He mediates the powers of being which are concentrated in him. He has them within himself in knowledge and he transforms them in action.[41]

What we can know from the above paragraph is that courage in Tillich's theology means the root of the human mind. Tillich does not enunciate that "courage" is created by external things, but it is created by something, and it resides in human minds. But Tillich mentions that even though the definition of Enlightment and the Romantic show "courage," it is not a desirable courage. So Tillich suggests that the genuine definition of courage is profoundly described in existentialism. This definition of courage in existentialism is the most influential and effective to understanding human beings. Tillich believes that "existentialism" is the most radical pattern of the courage to be oneself. "Existentialism" represents the most clear and threatening message of "existential." "Existentialism" implies, in Tillich's theology, first, that it is the expression of human anxiety about meaninglessness. Secondly, it is an attempt to take the human anxiety toward the courage to be human beings.

Tillich indicates why human beings fall into this meaninglessness: Objects which are created by human beings have replaced humans' inner selves and objects become subjective for human beings. But he believes that human beings do not have exits to escape or overcome this meaninglessness. They just strive to exit from this anxiety. This type of escape has been shown through art, existentialist philosophy, and literature. The reason humans can react to this kind of action is that we are not totally separated from the ontological root. Realizing one's existential situation implies that there are roots which still strive to recover the image of God. All kinds of existential anxiety point out that they have root in human beings, which cannot be verified visibly but testifies to the existence of itself through humans' existential anxiety. In this point, Tillich mentions the following:

> The courage to take upon oneself the loneliness of such anxiety and the horror of such vision is an outstanding expression of the courage to be as oneself. Man is separated from the sources of courage-but not completely: he is still able to face and to accept his own separation.[42]

The reason why people want to live meaningful lives and develop and challenge the meaning of their lives at mid-life is due to the archetypal image of God. In other words, the tendencies of generativity, which can be named as the successful sublimate of male mid-life crisis, come to blossom from the root, the archetypal image of God. In this sense Carl Jung believes that mid-lifers are supposed to encounter the unconscious, and this encounter brings out the "reformation" of a prior archetype, and this archetype cannot be distinguished from the image of God.[43] Jungian psychologist Edward Edinger defines the self in terms of the archetypal image of God.

> It was Jung's further discovery that the archetypal psyche has a structuring or ordering principle which unifies the various archetypal contents. This is the central archetype or archetype of wholeness which Jung has termed the Self...The Self is most simply described as the inner empirical deity and is identical with the *imago Dei*.[44]

What we have to remember is that this courage in Tillich's theology does not mean that it has sufficient ability to solve human existential anxiety, but strives to figure out the problems of human existentialism. Courage is striving which does not want to live without meaning. Tillich describes how human beings can have this courage to overcome their non-being. Tillich argues that there is an inseparable association between faith and courage.[45] In this perspective, he thinks that "faith" is the bridge which can combine the finite with the infinite. "Faith" leads people to union with the ground of being. In other words, courage is due to faith and the reason humans can have faith is that they have a deep relation with "the ground of being." As I mentioned in previous pages this theological perspective about "faith" can be related to the archetypal image of God. Thus, the reason human beings can ask ontological questions at mid-life against the threat of non-being, such as death, is due to this courage based on faith associated with the archetypal image of God. And this archetypal image of God at mid-life can appear as "generativity" in one's practical life as Erikson defines it. Because of this, people are challenged to sublimate their existential anxiety into creative works. In other words, as males approach mid-life they experience the finitude of human beings and realize that they are mortals. But in spite of feeling the limits, which are experienced existentially, simultaneously they desire immortality, because ontologically they are connected with Being-itself. Carl Jung believes that this intensive encounter with the image of God happens in the second half of life.[46]

David Gutmann's research on male tendencies after mid-life gives psychological understanding. David Gutmann,[47] whose work is based on

Jung's theory, researched men's psychological tendencies globally in Kansas City, Navajo, Druze, and Mayan culture. He found that as males grow old, starting in their middle age, they become more nurturing and caring.

> In brief, men who were once adversarial, whether as warriors, slash-and-burn agriculturalists, passionate pioneers, politicians, or trial lawyers, routinely become more pacific in later life, they turn to preserving life rather than killing, to maintaining social stability rather than fomenting ardent rebellion.[48]

He researched painters, such as George Price (born in 1901), William Steig (born in 1907), Edward Hopper (1882-1969), and Jean-Augusten-Dominique Ingres (1780-1867), and their paintings. George Price was a cartoonist. Sixty percent of his cartoons, which were drawn between the ages of 30 and 49, focused on males outdoors in competition. But as he approached age fifty a striking transition happened. Two-thirds of his drawings after age fifty were concerned with indoor things.[49] William Steig, in his middle years, did not accept the peculiarity of man as aggression, but as caring and concern. The themes of this drawings were caring and nurturing in his mid-life.

> ... he rejects the aggressive versions of masculinity, in his middle years Steig also seems to be troubled by an emerging feminity.....In other words, having put aside the idea of aggressive masculinity Steig discovers - like his age mates around the planet, and with a kind of horror - a hidden quality of softness and femininity at the very core of self. In him, we see the conflicts over emerging androgyny that are generic to his midlife period.[50]

Edward Hopper worked as painter for ninety years, from his youth until his death. In his young periods the themes of his painting were about powerful machines such as locomotives, tugboats, etc. But, in his mid-life, his drawings changed to the domestic world of houses. One of his famous paintings drawn in his middle age is a White Victorian House which shows a lonely scene of the house. As he approached middle age, his concern for painting changed into the domestic interior rather than the exterior.[51] Jean-Augusten-Dominique Ingres was a French painter in the 19th century. Comparing his paintings in young age in which he usually painted land battles, sea battles and heros, his paintings of after middle age focused on the "woman-filled domestic interior," in which women became the true themes,[52] which indicates caring, nurturing and reconciliation. What David Gutmann concludes from his research about the four painters is as follows:

> In their rendition of space across the life span, these four artists have traced out a clear human universal. Whether cartoonists or fine artist, whether French or American, whether of this century or another, as male artists age they migrate in their creations away from boundless outer space, away from the domain of the perimeter and large, thrusting, exploratory movement; instead they carve out their claim to the interior.[53]

Gutmann also shows Joseph Carnon's research (1982) about divorce lawyers. Joseph Carnon divided the lawyers into two age groups: younger lawyers and lawyers after mid-life. Most younger lawyers' concerns were with how to win lawsuits. They did not care about family reunion and reconciliation. Rather they had a concern to win lawsuits. But lawyers who were aged had a strong concern for reconciliation, reunion, their family and children rather than winning lawsuits. Their roles were as counselors who tried to reconcile these things.[54] Gutmann's research provides us with some clues for understanding the male psyche tendency which seeks some integration, combination, and caring for next generation, starting in middle age, and directly verifies how the self as the archetypal image of God emerges at mid-life. What he concludes from these researches is that the tendency to be peace-maker, pacifier, reconciler, counselor and caring for community and the next generation is not limited to a specific person or area. It can occur without connection to jobs, races, and territories.[55]

Tillich also emphasizes the centered self, which only human beings have. But Tillich's theology does not overlook the human existential problems of the self as we receive his concept of the self. As Tillich's theology focuses on the existential problems of human beings and the ontological essence of being human, his dialogue with psychology as human science suggests the existential limitations of the self. In order to talk about human existential problems Tillich starts the dialogue by defining three categories of human beings. Theologically speaking, he divides humans' situations into three categories: creation, the Fall, and salvation.[56] What Tillich believes is that if people do not see these three categories they cannot understand human beings. Based on these three categories he dialogues between theology and psychology. In terms of the three theological insights on human beings, he indirectly criticizes the inflated concept of human potentialities. In other words, he does not deny the potentialities of human beings, but he criticizes tendencies which do not observe the existential estrangements of the self, such as unbelief, hubris and concupiscence, which we can encounter as self-absorption/stagnation. Tillich's theological concept of the image of God supports concretely this concept of the human self. In defining the image of God, Tillich argues that it has two implications: *imago* and *similitudo*. These two terms have been used for defining the image of God. First *imago* points to the natural equipment of humans, and, secondly, *similitudo* means a special divine gift, which was endowed to Adam so he could associate with God.

> Man as creature has been called the "image of God."...The discussion is complicated by the fact that the biblical report uses two terms for this idea, which were translated as *imago* and *similitudo*. These were distinguished in their meaning(Irenaeus). *Imago* was supposed to point to the natural equipment of man; *similitudo*, to the special divine gift, the *donum superadditum*, which gave Adam the power of adhering to God.[57]

Tillich insists that the states of *imago* and *similitudo* are possible in the stage of human's pure nature. In this stage human beings have the ability not only for communion with God but also with other creatures. But this state has been lost since the Fall. Because of this current state of human beings, we are in "dreaming innocence" in which we dream innocence, but as soon as it actualizes we will not experience essence but existence, estrangement from innocence. In this point, Tillich's theological understanding of the image of God, which I compare with the archetypal image of God, which can be expressed as creative works, caring for others, community concerns, etc. in the perspective of *generativity* at mid-life, shows that generative tendencies at mid-life imply nostalgia to be reunited with God. But, in detail, Tillich does not think that by this tendency human beings can be recovered from their estrangement. I think of this generative tendency as nothing but a nostalgia to miss "dreaming innocence." Thus, theologically speaking, this generative tendency or the archetypal image of God as the centered self can be experienced when we encounter the Divine Spirit who shakes, transforms our beings and brings healing to male mid-lifers.[58]

A Critical Dialogue of Psychology and Theology on Male Mid-life Crisis

In the above discussion I have researched the cause of male midlife crisis in the perspectives of Erikson's concept of generativity and stagnation, Jung's life cycle theory, and contemporary psychologists. According to Carl Jung the cause of mid-life crisis is due to the psyche's movement which wants to recover and encounter the archetypal image of God. This archetype, as Jung mentioned, cannot be destroyed and annihilated by any external milieu, because it is an instinct. In the same vein, Erikson argues that generativity is an instinct. And Don Browning mentions that it is an archaic unconscious. What is common among these psychologists is that this tendency is supposed to happen at mid-life.

As I mentioned in chapter 2 Jung indicates that according to the principle of the second half of life one is supposed to live based on the spiritual life. In other words, male mid-life identity/crisis is a stage in which males are supposed to seek the meaning and value of their lives. I define it as the "religious tendency" in male mid-life identity/crisis. This religious tendency in mid-life is an initiative stage to enter exocentrical concerns such as caring for future generations, community, etc. So egocentrical tendencies in the first half of life have been challenged by exocentrical tendencies at mid-life. As it were, males in this stage are supposed to think about what is most valuable in life because of the archetypal image of God. But what we have a problem about in the archetypal image of God is that even though archetype is an instinct which cannot be destroyed and erased by any conditions, we live in modernity which hardly supports the role of this archetype. Materialistic and capitalistic milieu force us to see only one side of life, not spirituality. Because of this we pursue the aims of individual goals based on egoism, which has shaped human mentality and the value of individuals. We are absorbed in so-called narcissistic individualism. In this sense a research result proves that the experience of stagnation has been increasing, comparing the past with the present.[59] In this perspective modern people have forgotten and disregarded the meaning of the Spirit which is the crucial element for later stages of their life cycle. In this lopsided and unbalanced environment it is not easy to experience the positive result of male mid-life crisis in terms of archetype because of social milieus. Instead we have experienced a desperate experience of life and stagnation, such as destruction, killing, abandoning one's family, etc. From these desperate and egocentrical experiences I cannot help feeling the neglected archetypal image of God. Theologically speaking, I feel that we need some reality which can stimulate human beings to be transformed and which can help to recover the archetypal image of God, which is ontologically connected with the Spirit but existentially now has been oppressed and hidden by social and individual milieus. Regarding this question, Tillich's theology suggests that the Spiritual Presence can liberate the oppressed and neglected archetypal image of God. These theological reflections of Tillich on the Spiritual Presence and "New Being" provide a theological dialogue with psychological perspectives on male mid-life identity/crisis, because Tillich's theology points out the limitation of psychological interpretations on the archetype and suggests a theological solution for the self at mid-life.

I need to mention again the meaning of "New Being" because it is essential to this critical dialogue between psychology and theology on male mid-life crisis. Tillich indicates that desiring "New Being" is a universal ontological question to humanity. And this implies a desire to be in a transformed reality from the old being. Tillich points out that this ontological anxiety of human beings to experience "New Being" can be addressed by realizing the limitations of the self. It can happen because we are conscious of being limited and determined in our nature. Tillich indicates that this ability to know human limitation is a result of the spirit in humanity. Ontological anxieties and sufferings occurring in male mid-life crisis happen because of the spirit of humanity. In other words, psychologically speaking, in a Jungian perspective, the anxieties come from the archetypal image of God, which experiences tensions between human ontological desires and its existential situations.

The quest for the New Being is universal because the human predicament and its ambiguous conquest are universal. We need to understand the difference between psychological understanding and theological understanding about mid-life crisis. First of all, Carl Jung insists that the loss of spiritual center is associated with the mid-life crisis. In this sense he tried to heal his mid-life patients in terms of approaching the center of inherent mode of psyche.[60] In other words, because of the ego-centered tendency at mid-life mid-lifers are apt to fall in to aimlessness and meaninglessness of life, and therefore the urgent task for mid-lifers is to renew the priori archetype which is regarded as the image of God as the centered self.[61] Thus, Jung concludes that the results of this encounter with the unconscious as the archetypal image of God are faithful, trustful, and cooperative humanity among people.[62]

Murray Stein also indicates that the major cause of mid-life crisis is due to the neglected archetypal image of God although he accepts the influence of social milieu. So the purpose of the mid-life crisis is "a pilgrimage to recover the image of God,"and the result of encountering the archetypal image of God appears as an ethical obligation.[63] Erik Erikson regards the generative tendency as a human instinct, but it is also a natural result of interaction through a psychosocial development of oneself. And the result of generativity can appear as procreativity, productivity, and creativity. Erikson regards that "immortality" causes generativity at mid-life which is the nostalgia for immortality.[64] Daniel Levinson explains that mid-life crisis happens based on two elements: the self and the world. In other words, mid-life crisis can happen in terms of the interaction between the two elements. There are four polarities which affect the self. Among these Levinson regards that Young/Old polarity is the most important archetype which affects other polarities, it results from immortality which encompasses the other polarities. In this sense he believes that altruism becomes "a vehicle for the search for immortality," which is regarded as an ordinary human urge.[65] All these psychological interpretations and results of mid-life crisis are associated with "New Being" in Tillich's theology. If so, why do we want to experience "New Being"? In describing the meaning of death to humans, Tillich points out that this experience of death makes people experience as non-being and brings the cause of anxiety. As we realize the fear of death we are apt to fall in the meaninglessness of life, and this meaninglessness causes the problems of psyche.

> It is also clear that all existential utterances deal with the boundary line between healthy and sick and ask one question - you can reduce it to this - how is it possible that a being has a structure that produces psychosomatic deceases? Existentialism in order to answer these questions points to the possible experience of meaninglessness, to the continuous experience of loneliness, to the widespread feelings of emptiness. It derives them from finitude, from the awareness of finitude which is anxiety; it derives them from the possibility from oneself and one's world.[66]

Tillich emphasizes that all human anxieties, such as meaninglessness, emptiness, etc., bring out psychosomatic diseases. All human possibilities should be destroyed in terms of the experience because of these. In other words, all potentialities and possibilities of human beings disappear in the presence of death. Tillich articulates that existential anxiety comes in terms of this realization of the transitory moment of life.

> As experience in immediate self-awareness, time unites the anxiety of transitoriness with the courage of a self-affirming present. The melancholy awareness of the trend of being toward nonbeing, a theme which fills the literature of all nations, is most actual in the anticipation of one's own death. What is significant here is not the fear of death, that is, the moment of dying. It is anxiety of having to die which reveals the ontological character of time. In the anxiety of having to die nonbeing is experienced from "the inside." This anxiety is potentially present in every moment. It permeates the whole of man's being; it shapes soul and body and determines spiritual life.[67]

Tillich's description of anxiety of death has close parallels with the research of Daniel Levinson and Elliot Jaques. Levinson and his associates conclude that the major cause of mid-life identity/crisis comes from the experience of death, Young and Old polarity.[68] As they feel the limitation and finitude of human beings, males are supposed to reflect on the goal of their lives and how the goal has been achieved in the perspectives of meanings in their mid-life.

In understanding the potentialities of self, there is a big gap between Jung's understanding of archetype, possibility of image of God, and Tillich's understanding of the self. Even though Tillich accepts the potentiality of human being and its universal desire to be "New Being," he points out the limitations and ambiguities of human beings. In other words, Tillich realizes the gap between existential situations and ontological desires. The ultimate despair of human beings may result in a concern for New Being, but this concern cannot transform human beings even though it is a universal desire, because it is only desire. For instance, in describing the universal tendencies of centeredness, such as self-integration, he indicates negative result of self-integration. It is a "totalitarian ruler." Self-creativity of humans also has self-destruction. And self-transcendence implies the profanization which makes all subjects into objects.[69] In these perspectives, Tillich criticizes those who had optimistic perspectives on human nature, such as Erich Fromm and Carl Jung. According to Tillich:

> Men like Fromm speak of the possibility of becoming an

autonomous non-authoritarian personality who develops himself according to reason. And even Jung, who knows so much about the depths of the human soul and about the religious symbols, thinks that there are essential structures in the human soul and that it is possible(and one may be successful) to search for personality. In all these representatives of contemporary depth psychology we miss the depths of Freud. We miss the feeling for the irrational element that we have in Freud and in much of the existentialist literature.[70]

As an existential theologian what Tillich experienced from human potentialities was negative. One exemplary diary of Tillich shows his frustration about human nature. As he went through the experience of World Wars I and II, he experienced desperate potentialities of the human self. Tillich experiences the depravity and atrocity of human potentialities. After all, he believes that the depravity of human beings cannot be healed or overcome by humanistic methods and potentialities. Comparing Jung's concept of archetype with Tillich's theological interpretations of the self, Tillich indicates that the universal desire of human beings, "New Being," cannot be experienced in terms of human potentialities, even though it is a universal desire.[71]

In Jung's psychology, archetypes in the collective unconscious have been regarded as transcending space and time. These archetypes are absolute, which cannot be changed and transformed throughout human history. They are beyond time and space. Jung's theory of archetypes is a very influential theory to understand human beings, but it does not care about human milieu which is also a very crucial element to determining one's identity, as Erikson emphasized the role of social milieu toward one's identity formation. This point reflects why Jung's concept of archetype has been criticized because it disregards social contexts.[72] Thus, social context, which means successive good-enough developmental stages of life, is another crucial element which affects mid-life. In terms of our contemporary social values we are more connected in narcissistic society. How powerful is the influence of social milieu to individuals in contemporary society? The limitedness of human ability is explained through the concept of stagnation in Erikson's psychosocial theory and Donald Capps' detailed explanation of it in chapter 2. In other words, the universal desire of "New Being" can be hardly experienced in terms of the archetypal image of God, because it is a just desire which comes from the deep side of human psyche in male mid-life. So this desire is interrupted and frustrated by the ambiguities of the self and not good-enough social milieu. Thus, Tillich's theology suggests that the limitation of the self can be overcome in terms of the Spiritual Presence. According to Tillich, the Spiritual Presence brings out the meaning to human beings. In other words, the religious questions which occur at the male mid-life crisis can be answered by encountering the Spiritual Presence, because it bears the meaning of beings. As Tillich points out the Spiritual Presence, he emphasizes that it is not "an informative lesson about God and divine matter," but "a meaning-bearing power."[73]

The experience of the Spiritual Presence can stimulate and wake our potentiality of the archetypal image of God and bring a meaning for humans. In terms of this function, the Spiritual Presence can make mid-lifers experience "generative men/ new being" because it has a meaning-bearing power. But Tillich emphasizes that the encounter with the Spiritual Presence does not destroy human's rational nature. Rather it embraces it with its own depth and transcends it and shows a direction. He suggests that this tendency to live under the influence of the Spiritual Presence is the divine demand of "theonomy," and describes it in detail as follows:

> Theonomous culture is Spirit-determined and Spirit-directed culture, and Spirit fulfils spirit instead of breaking it. The idea of theonomy is not antihumanistic, but it turns the humanistic indefiniteness about the "where-to" into a direction which transcends every particular human aim.[74]

In other words, it is essential to experience the encounter with the Spirit in the second half of life because most mid-lifers are supposed to live based on spiritual perspectives. But the experience of the Spiritual Presence does not mean perfection. It is a partial experience of it. In talking about the experience of the Spiritual Presence, Tillich points out the momentary experience of it. In other words, the experience of the Spiritual Presence through mid-life crisis is crucial to finding one's ontological and religious meaning, but the experience of it is not permanent. It is a transitory experience which needs to be fulfilled continually through the conversion experience.[75] In this sense the encounter of Spiritual Presence is the inevitable stage to reaching the generative man or New Being at mid-life.

In conclusion, I think that male mid-life is a crucial period because male mid-lifers can broadly affect family and community positively or negatively. In this stage males are challenged by the neglected archetypal image of God which begins occurring at mid-life and asks the real values and meanings of life. This challenging stage is designed to be lived based on spiritual perspectives. But even though this kind of religious perspective occurring in mid-life is associated with the archetypal image of God, its results can be influenced in terms of one's social milieu, such as one's endeavors, family, education, community, etc. But what we worry is about our social milieu, which is not mature, to stimulate the renewal experience of archetype even though it is instinct. In this perspective, the more dangerous thing is that we have experienced frustration, atrocity, and despair through contemporary society. We are more self-centered than spiritual, and this tendency has replaced the genuine meaning of our lives. Most milieus, such as materialism and the value of life based on only reason, materialism and capitalism, have oppressed the archetypal image of God. Because of this challenge to male mid-lifers in the contemporary world it is hard to experience "generative men/ new being." Thus, to reactivate, liberate, and recover the archetypal image of God, males need to encounter the Spiritual Presence, because the experience of Spiritual Presence bears the meaning of life, as Tillich indicates. And we need some environment which encourages and formulates the reactivation of the archetypal image of God in terms of experiencing the Spiritual Presence. It is an urgent necessity for individuals, families, and society, because through this experience and encounter we can expect a generative man/religious man whose aims are not associated with egocentricity but exocentricity. In this perspective we need the healing process which reconciles the split self and the "Spiritual Presence." It means to open toward the Spiritual Presence to renew the archetypal image of God at the stage of male mid-life crisis. The Spiritual Presence can liberate the oppressed, hidden, and neglected archetypal image of God in terms of experiencing the Spiritual Presence who brings out the conversion experience. Thus, male mid-life identity/crisis and its theological dialogue shows the necessity of pastoral intervention through which men take steps toward "generative men/ new being" at mid-life.

(Notes)

1. Lewis R. Aiken, *Dying, Death and Bereavement* (Boston: Allyn and Bacon, 1994), 263-64.

2. Erik H. Erikson, *Childhood and Society* (New York: Norton and Company, 1985), 296.
3. Bert Hayslip Jr. and Paul E. Panek, *Adult Development and Aging* (New York: Harper Collins College Publishers, 1993), 490.
4. Paul Tillich, *Courage To Be* (New Haven & London: Yale University Press, 1952), 36-54.
5. Ibid., 30.
6. *ST.* Vol. 1, 198.
7. Ibid., 189.
8. *ST.* Vol. 2, 186.
9. *ST.* Vol. 1, 186.
10. Ibid., 163.
11. Ibid., 191.
12. *ST.* Vol. 2, 49.
13. *ST.* Vol. 1, 192.
14. Ibid., 193.
15. Ibid., 195.
16. Ibid.
17. Ibid., 196.
18. Ibid.
19. Ibid.
20. *ST.* Vol.1, 197-98.
21. Paul Tillich, *Courage To Be,* 36-52.
22. *ST.* Vol. 2, 191-92.
23. *ST.* Vol. 1, 191.
24. Daniel Levinson, op. cit., 222.
25. Ibid., 89-90.
26. Ibid., 90.
27. Erik H. Erikson, *Vital Involvement in Old Age* (New York and London: Norton, 1985), 74-75; And see the Chapter 2.
28. Erik Erikson, *Childhood and Society*, 267; Daniel Levinson, op. cit., 219.
29. *ST.* Vol. 2, 49-50.
30. Ibid., 188.
31. Ibid., 201.
32. Alexander J. McKelway, *The Systematic Theology of Paul Tillich* (New York: Delta Book, 1964), 132.
33. *ST.* Vol. 1, 209.
34. Ibid., 206.
35. Ibid., 198.
36. Robert L. Moore & Douglas Gillette, *The King Within: Accessing the King in Male Psyche* (New York: William Morrow and Company Inc., 1992), 202.
37. Paul Tillich, "Carl Jung," in *The Meaning of Health: Essays in Existentialism, Psychoanalysis, and Religion*, 176.
38. Paul Tillich, *Courage To Be*, 116.
39. Ibid.
40. Ibid., 120.

41. Ibid.
42. Ibid., 144.
43. *CW.*, 9-2, 40.
44. Edward F. Edinger, *Ego and Archetype: Individuation and the Religious Function of the Psyche* (Boston & London: Shambhala, 1972), 3.
45. Paul Tillich, *Courage To Be,* 172.
46. Edward Edinger, op. cit., 4.
47. Emeritus Professor of Psychiatry Education and Director of the Older Adult Psychology at Northwestern University.
48. David Gutmann, *Reclaimed Powers: Men and Women in Later Life* (Evanston, IL: Northwestern University Press, 1994), 94.
49. Ibid., 76.
50. Ibid., 74.
51. Ibid., 78-79.
52. Ibid., 80.
53. Ibid., 81.
54. Ibid.,94.
55. Ibid.
56. Ibid., 87.
57. *ST.* Vol. 1, 258.
58. *ST.* Vol. 3, 167.
59. John Korte, *Outliving the Self: How we live on in future generations* (New York & London: W. W. Norton Company, 1994),1-2.
60. *CW.* Vol. 7, 138.
61. *CW.* Vol. 9-2, 40.
62. *CW.* Vol. 7, 173-74.
63. Murray Stein, In Midlife: A Jungian Perspective (Dallas Texas: Spring Texas, Spring Publication),124.
64. Erik Erikson, *Vital Involvement in Old Age*, 74-75.
65. Daniel Levinson, op.cit., 219.
66. Paul Tillich,*The Meaning of Health: Essays in Existentialism, Psychoanalysis, and Religion*, 86.
67. *ST.* Vol. 1, 193-94.
68. See Chapter 3.
69. See chapter 4.
70. Paul Tillich, "The Theological Significance of Existentialism and Psychoanalysis," in *The Meaning of Health: Essays in Existentialism, Psychoanalysis, and Religion*, 90.
71. *ST.* Vol. 3, 86-87.
72. Demariss S. Wehr, *Jung & Feminism: Liberating Archetypes* (Boston: Beacon Press, 1987), 103-14.
73. *ST.* Vol. 3, 155.
74. Ibid., 250.
75. Ibid., 140.

Chapter 6

Conclusion: Pastoral Implications and Interventions for Male Mid-life Crisis

Pastoral Analysis for Male Mid-life Crisis and Its Implication

Donald Capps defines the goal of pastoral care for mid-lifers as being "to facilitate their desire to replace the dream of their young adulthood with a vision more appropriate to the 'transformed narcissism of middle adulthood.'" More concretely speaking, he suggests three goals of pastoral counseling in Levinsonian perspectives for mid-lifers as follows: the purpose is "to foster the restructuring of their perceptions of themselves, of other persons, and of the world around them." Generally he believes that male mid-lifers are more concerned with how to become more self-directed and much more concerned with how to become a more "whole" person and how to perceive the world more "wholly" or "fully." In this sense, in a Christian context, he thinks that the purpose of pastoral counseling for mid-lifer is to make "the responsible self," "the believable self," and "the accessible self."[1] But, in contrast, Capps points out that the dominant personality of modern society manipulates personal relationships, controls people, and makes people serve their own goals. In this sense, he indicates the necessity of "the responsible self," "the believable self," and "the accessible self" for mid-lifers. These three important concepts of the self are regarded as "a perception of oneself as symbolic of the Eternal Self," which is formed in the image of God.[2] But he insists that a transforming experience of pastoral counseling can be realized by "replacing oneself as the center of one's existence with God, who is the Eternal Self." In this sense Capps suggests that as we place God as the center we can experience a good result for mid-life crisis.

> From the religious perspective represented here(i.e. the Judaeo-Christian tradition), this can only be realized by replacing oneself as the center of one's existence with God, who is the Eternal Self. This is the necessary perceptual restructuring that needs to occur before a transfer from self-love to object love can become a realistic love.[3]

According to Donald Capps, deep-rooted stagnation in terms of egoism appears as unconcern and indifference about others. In a pastoral psychological perspective, Capps explains that such egoism in mid-life is intensively associated with narcissism. And those who have narcissistic personalities manipulate the relationship between themselves and others in order to accomplish their interests.[4] As a result, such a narcissistic personality expects a desirable consequence through an excessive tenacity of purpose for oneself, and it brings out the destruction of oneself, others, and God.

What is the pastoral psychological analysis regarding why people are bound in stagnation? William Barry points out the reason people are excessively attached to stagnation is that we are ignorant of our reality and limitations. Senselessness about the reality of ourselves, and insensibility and indifference regarding God, it becomes social malaise which hinders for identifying oneself in contemporary society.[5] If we fall into amnesia about our limitations and tend to apathy toward God, we begin to be indifferent to concerns of generativity which results in stagnation in terms of self-absorption, egoism.

Carl G. Jung's reflections about patients who visited him while they were middle aged implies that much of human mid-life struggle is related to humans' unconscious desire for seeking meaning from aimlessness and meaninglessness. He also mentioned that the patients' sufferings were associated with religious meanings. Thus, most patients who visited Carl Jung because of mid-life identity/crisis solved their problems through religious meanings. Howard Clinebell indicates that those who are in mid-life have been so challenged through human limitations such as death, and physical and mental enervation that "spiritual issues" are very important for them.[6] These "spiritual issues" are related to *faith*. John Shea points out that there is an intimate relationship between faith and mid-life. In this sense, he argues that what is crucial for mid-lifers is how can we plant mature faith through which they may have a chance to rehabilitate their identities through others and

God.[7] Furthermore, he insists that religious experience is the most important element for mid-lifers because mid-lifers can have a chance to reconstruct and transform their identity through the religious experience.[8]

Male Mid-life Crisis and Spirituality

In the previous pages, I point out that the spiritual encounter with God is essential for the pastoral counseling of male mid-lifers. In this part, I will explore concretely what "'religious experience" means and how it relates to pastoral counseling for male mid-lifers. In the pastoral perspective, Donald Capps analyzes how the meaning of stagnation in mid-life is related to religious experience and spiritual crisis as follows:

> Acedia(Stagnation) is a spiritual crisis, and the only solution to the crisis is a spiritual renewal through which the spirit of God moves within us and moves us to care again. On the other hand, though we cannot force the spirit to move within us and restore us to life again, we can open ourselves to the spirit and be receptive to it.[9]

What Capps describes to solve mid-lifers' stagnation is to experience spiritual renewal through which we will experience the transformation process of the self; this process makes mid-lifers experience and realize what "care" is. This care means to take care of oneself, others and God. According to Capps, the only way to experience God is to open our mind toward God, and then we can experience a spiritual renewal. But we cannot control the spirit of God. We are not directors who can control the spirit of God but recipients. In this sense we need to open ourselves to experience the renewal of the centered self. Renewal means to awaken the hidden, oppressed, and repressed image of God in terms of encountering the spirit of God. And then what does it mean to "open to God?" "Open to God" connotes giving up one's previous thinking and patterns of life, and desiring a new dimension of thinking and patterns of life. Henry Nouwen provides more implications about what is openness in a theological perspective.

> This openness, however, does not simply come of itself. It requires our confession that we are limited, dependent, weak, and even sinful. Whenever you pray, you profess that you are not God and

that you wouldn't want to be, that you haven't reached your goal yet, and that you never will reach it in this life, that you must constantly stretch out your hands and wait again for the gift which gives new life. This attitude is difficult because it makes you vulnerable.[10]

As long as we have the image of God, we need to be open to God. Openness to God means to be ready to be transformed from one's self-centeredness tendencies such as being aggressive and destructive against oneself, others, and God, and expect a transformed self and reconstructed self, characterized by caring, intimacy, empathy toward oneself, others, and God. Psychologically speaking, we accept the vanity and meaninglessness of the first half of life and open our hearts to the Spirit who renews, guides and works in the second half of life. This is called a "conversion" experience among religious experiences. As we have this conversion experience we can feel and experience the renewal of the repressed, oppressed, and hidden archetypal image of God. In terms of this we may start the transformation process of generative men. We can find another exemplary story from the conversation between Nicodemus and Jesus in the Bible.

> Now there was a Pharisee named Nicodemus, a leader of the Jews. He came to Jesus by night and said to him, "Rabbi, we know that you are a teacher who has come from God; for no one can do these signs that you do apart from the presence of God." Jesus answered him, "Very truly, I tell you, no one can see the kingdom of God without being born from above." Nicodemus said to him, "How can anyone be born after having grown old? Can one enter a second time into the mothers' womb and be born? Jesus answered, "Very truly, I tell you, no one can enter the kingdom of God without being born of water and Spirit. What is born of the flesh is flesh, and what is born of the Spirit is spirit. Do not be astonished that I said to you, 'You must be born from above.' The wind blows where it chooses, and you hear the sound of it, but you do not know where it comes from or where it goes. So it is with everyone who is born of the Spirit." Nicodemus said to him, "How can these things be?" Jesus answered him, "Are you a teacher of Israel, and yet you do not understand these things? (NRSV, John 3: 1-10).

Raymond Studzinski insists that although the term mid-life identity/crisis is a contemporary one, the phenomena of mid-life crisis has continued through all ages and countries.[11] In this sense, the questions raised by Nichodemus and the answers given by Jesus, which happened about 2000 years in a geographically different place, remind us of the importance of mid-life crisis. The above story shows us indirectly the relationship between mid-life crisis and spiritual renewal. From my perspective, this is a story of male mid-life. The story of Nicodemus and answers of Jesus reflect that human beings need to be born again. I think that Jesus gave two essential comments to Nicodemus. First is "...no one can see the kingdom of God without being born from above," and then second one is "what is born to the flesh is flesh, and what is born of the Sprit is spirit." The meaning "born from above" implicates transformation, and the foundation of it comes from the experience of conversion. In other words, although we have explored optimistic values in psychological perspectives about the archetypal image of God as the centered self, there is something which needs to understand and experience precedently. It means that without encountering the Spirit of God, which results in a transformative process that separates oneself from one's previous patterns of life, the patterns of the first half of life, it is hard to experience a spiritual renewal. The encounter with the Spirit of God, which guides mid-lifers to the conversion experience, gives us a concern to take the process of generative men. So, Studzinski points out that the experience of conversion means having a new relationship with oneself, others, and God.[12] In this sense the most crucial and important element for male mid-life crisis is to experience the transformation process in terms of a conversion experience to experience a transformed reality. So mid-life is a good period to experience the image of God in terms of a conversion experience.[13] Donald Capps believes that the conversion experience had previously been importantly regarded for adolescence. But as we experience the rapid cultural change of contemporary society, the conversion experience needs to be especially emphasized for adults in mid-life.[14] We need to understand attentively regarding what is conversion through James Fowler's definition.

> Conversion means a release from the burden of self-groundness...It means embracing the conviction that we are known, loved, supported, and invited to partnership in being with One, who form all eternity intended us and who desires our love and partnership. Conversion means a recentering of our passion...Conversion means a realignment of our affections, the restructuring of our virtues, and the growth in lucidity and power of our partnership with God's work

in the world.[15]

What I want to say about conversion is not whether conversion is a dramatic experience or a result of ongoing process through education. My focus is that the experience of conversion cannot be considered to be once in a life time, but needs to be continued because it is a process of transformation to be the generative man. Conversion is the first step which can engender and awaken our repressed, oppressed, and hidden primordial image of God. The continuing conversion process in terms of committing to the vertical dimension makes us to be known to God, to be beloved, to be valuable beings and to be a partner to form the generative world.

In a pastoral theological perspective, openness to God at mid-life means openness toward "Ultimate Concern." The optimistic result, generative men, of "Ultimate Concern" can be engendered as we open our mind to it. The phenomenon of encountering "Ultimate Concern" is to reconcile oneself with one's self-alienation, others, and God. And all those reconciliations can bring out a reality of hope, reunion and reconciliation.[16] The reason we can experience the renewal phenomena from the broken relationships is that God has a capacity for reconciliation and renewal. In this sense, Tillich argues how much the meaning of "Ultimate Concern" takes the crucial role in pastoral counseling as follows:

> Counseling is another element in the same reality. It deals with special forms of psychological disturbances and human relationship in which these disturbances occur. And pastoral counseling deals with them in relations to an *ultimate concern* and not in relation to preliminary concerns, as for instance social and psychological and bodily health. This is the difference between the kinds of functions.[17]

So the major purpose of pastoral counseling in Tillich's perspective is to invite counselees to "Ultimate Concern" to experience "New Being," which means the *generative man* in a psychological term. The invitation to "Ultimate Concern" in pastoral counseling means to invite counselees to experience "New Being" by reflecting on their mid-life crisis based on "Ultimate Concern." Donald Capps in his article "Pastoral Counseling for Middle Adults" argues that the faith about "Ultimate Concern" can provide a good result for mid-life crisis. According to Donald Capps, as long as mid-lifers are not concerned about the Eternal Self, God, it is impossible to experience the transformation from self-love, *stagnation*, to object love, *generativity*, because of intensive attachment to self-centeredness at mid-life, which results in stagnation and hinders the discovery and realization of the true meaning of mid-life crisis. In other words, self-love or self-absorption, the typical tendency of mid-life, can be transformed to object-love, the tendency of generative men, as it is replaced by the Eternal Self, God. This is exactly the same as the implied meaning of conversion. In this sense, I think that the purpose of pastoral counseling for male mid-lifers is to support them to experience the transformation stage of generative men in terms of experiencing the Spirit of God. By replacing our self-centered tendencies through encountering the Spirit we start a transformative journey from self-love to object love.

Conclusive Suggestions: Pastoral Counseling As Spiritual Direction for Recovering the Centered Self

In pervious parts I have explored that for male mid-lifers crisis is intimately associated with spiritual dimensions. Existential psychotherapist Viktor Frankle asserts that the spiritual dimension is the most necessary element in the process of therapy because human beings themselves consist of spiritual dimensions. Thus, counseling therapy should start with curing the human spirit in the perspective of spiritual dimensions.[18] This type of general counseling appears not only in therapy, but also in counseling ministries where we have encountered many counselees and clients who want to be counseled in the perspective of spirituality.[19] Furthermore, I think that spirituality can take an important part for counseling of male mid-lifers because pastoral counseling for male mid-life crisis is deeply connected with religious meanings. So it is an inseparable relation between pastoral counseling and spirituality, because it is reciprocal. At this point, pastoral counseling can be considered as one of the spiritual directions.[20] In a sense, the pastoral counseling concern for mid-life crisis is a type of modern pietism because this pastoral counseling is intimately associated with spirituality.[21]

> As spiritual direction helps counselees to be able to relate and respond to God and be able to live in God, pastoral care has the same purpose. In this sense, the reason pastoral counseling is, in a

traditional sense, a spiritual direction that is a form of pastoral counseling.[22]

As Kenneth Leech defines spirituality, he explains the relationship between spirituality and pastoral care as follows:

> What then is spiritual direction? It is a relationship of friendship in Christ between two people by which one is enabled through the personal encounter, to discern more clearly the will of God for one's life, and to grow in discipleship and in the life of grace.[23]

In other words, a director of spiritual direction is supposed to lead counselees toward the right relationship with God, and help counselees understand and realize what is God's will for them. In this perspective, the main purpose of spiritual direction is to guide and help counselees to have an intimate relationship with God, and help them respond to God in terms of this relationship. Thus, the main goal of pastoral counseling for male mid-lifers is to help them to live and respond to the archetypal image of God as the centered self in terms of spiritual encounter with the Spirit. Kevin Culligan in his article "The Counseling Ministry and Spiritual Direction," emphasizes the intimate relationship between spirituality and pastoral counseling as follows:

> If we view our counseling ministry as the Church's attempt to help all her people grow in all their relationships, then spiritual direction, which concentrates on the person's relationship with God, coordinates with other specialities such as psychotherapy, group therapy, marriage and family counseling, crisis counseling, and career guidance where the focus is on the person's relationship with others, things, or events. In this view, the spiritual director is a counselor in the Church whose primary focus is helping persons grow in their relationship with God through prayer.[24]

What Culligan wants to emphasize in the above paragraph is that spiritual direction has such similar purposes with pastoral counseling that spiritual direction can help mid-life counselees. If so, how does the understanding of human psyche, psychological understandings about persons, help this spiritual direction? Can it be a tool to understand and help counselees for pastoral counseling? Regarding this question, Kenneth Leech explains as follows:

It would be as mistaken to see the spiritual guide as a therapist as it would be to place the 'spiritual' and the 'psychological' in entirely separate compartments. Spiritual direction necessarily involves the psyche: it enters the areas of psychological disturbance and psychological health; it concerns itself with issues of distress, inner conflict and upheaval, and mental pain.[25]

Leech accentuates that pastoral counseling or spiritual direction never excludes psychological compartments for effective counseling. Thus, in other words, psychological understandings about human development, psychopathology, etc., have a reciprocal relationship with pastoral counseling. I would like to suggest four necessary elements in order to have effective pastoral counseling for male mid-life crisis.

Psychoanalytic Understandings of Male Mid-life Crisis

Usually, one of the basic reasons why counselees ask for pastoral care givers or counselors is that they expect them to be religious guides. In this sense, pastoral counselors can be sure that religious faith and life have affected counselees whether counselees have developed a mature faith journey or not. It is a matter of course that "faith"takes an important role in pastoral counseling. Thus, it is inevitable to emphasize the unique relation of God as the third party in pastoral counseling. If so, how can pastoral counseling help male mid-lifers find true meanings as generative men? Regarding this challenging question, first of all, I want to research what types of qualifications are needed for effective pastoral counseling, because I consider that the qualifications of pastoral counselors take important roles for pastoral interventions.

For effective pastoral counseling, pastoral counselors need to prepare themselves to understand three things: God, persons, and their relationship.[26] In these perspectives, first, pastoral counselors have to have some qualified understandings of the psychological developments and phenomena of male mid-life. Due to their psychological understanding, pastoral counselors can more effectively counsel on the reasons for mid-life crisis. This psychological understanding about male mid-life does not only provide pastoral counselors with psychological motivations and psychopathology, but also psychological tools to understand counselees' situations. The understanding of counselees' psychological situations can help pastoral counselors analyze the relation of God to them.[27] Surely, as I mentioned, the counseling in pastoral ministries cannot help both associated with spirituality. But the psychological understanding, such as knowing the primary causes of male mid-life crisis, can help pastoral counselors understand what are the spiritual problems of counselees. In this sense, if pastoral counselors do not heed psychological understandings about mid-life, which has a reciprocal relationship with spirituality, pastoral counselors limit indiscriminately counselees' inner problems to other issues. This type of pastoral counselor loses a tool among two necessary tools for pastoral counseling, as Kenneth Leech indicates. As a result, because this pastoral counseling does not understand what kind of psychological situations exist for mid-lifers and what types of situations give them difficulty, the counseling becomes ineffective. In other words, psychological understanding about male mid-life is the bridge and the mediator to spirituality. Thus, in terms of understanding counselees' psychological situations and situations of living, pastoral counselors can provide them with effective counseling.

Vertical Dimension to Pastoral Counselor

Secondly, pastoral counselors need sufficiently pertinent faith for pastoral counseling. Through the experience of pastoral counseling Paul W. Pruyer describes why people want pastoral counseling as follows:

> I am convinced that a great many persons who turn to their pastor for help in solving personal problems seek assistance in some kind of religious or moral self-evaluation. They want to see some criteria of their faith applied to themselves.[28]

The main reason why counselees want pastoral counseling is that they want to expect and seek religious and spiritual guides to understand their problems. Kevin Culligan points out that this type of phenomena does not stop in general counseling but also in pastoral counseling.[29] In this sense, pastoral counselors are asked to have mature faith, which means an intimate relationship between oneself, others and God, because counselees can disclose and reveal their inner world when they feel that pastoral counselors have mature faith.[30] If pastoral counselors do not have the mature faith to help counselees, pastoral counselees cannot formulate therapeutic and safe milieus for counselees.[31] I think that this

Conclusion: Pastoral Implications and Interventions 141

vertical dimension with God to pastoral counselors is the most essential element because of the peculiar characteristic of pastoral counseling. So, the experiential awareness of God's presence should be a main element for any pastoral counselor.[32] In this perceptive, Kenneth Leech emphasizes as follows how much pastoral counselors' spiritual devotional life is crucial in guiding others and pastoral counseling.

> If we are to provide the future church which pastors who are capable of guiding others, we need to place a very high priority indeed on training in prayers, on the practice of silence and reflection, on deepening the awareness of the presence of God, on helping people to understand the principles of spiritual growth, and on placing all theological work within a framework of worship and prayer.[33]

This devotional and spiritual life of pastoral counselors is the difference between general counseling and pastoral counseling. In general, counselors do not focus on counselees' ultimate concerns or fundamental questions, but concentrate on counselees' immediate problems. It may be true that religious values and meanings can be talked about in general counseling, but religious or spiritual concerns are not the main intention in general counseling. Conversely speaking, even in pastoral counseling, pastoral counselors need a psychological understanding of and knowledge about counselees. If pastoral counselors focus only on psychological understandings about counselees, they cannot provide effective pastoral counseling, because most pastoral counselees' intention to visit pastoral counselors indicate an expectation of religious and spiritual insights. Thus this vertical dimension of pastoral counseling reflects theological implications for pastoral counselors. Tillich mentions the importance of the vertical dimension to pastoral counseling as follows:

> Wherever a minister gives counsels, he should do it in the light of the eternal...He should be aware that functionally he represents the church, that he represents the New Being, in spite of its ambiguity, and that this representation makes him perform a function different from the others.[34]

In this sense, pastoral counseling happens in a prepared divine dimension between pastoral counselors and counselees. Thus, pastoral counseling needs to be accomplished in divine frameworks and perspectives beyond psychological understandings and counseling skills.

Pastoral counselors are not only required to observe counselees' current psychological situations, but also need to help and guide them spiritual insights to see their situations beyond present problems. Pastoral counseling does not emphasize a temporary solution and guide to counselees but focuses on total values.[35] Pastoral counselors need to guide counselees to God beyond the self, because of the intimate connection with pastoral counseling and divine dimension. So, pastoral counselors need to practice personal communication with God.[36] This practice for self-communication with God is a discipline to pastoral counselors as general counselors have their own practice.

Empathic Spirituality as Image of God

Thirdly, pastoral counselors need to have *emphatic spirituality* for counselees. Whereas spiritual dimensions mean a vertical dimension between pastoral counselors and God, this third one is a horizontal dimension with counselees. I want to call this horizontal dimension "emphatic spirituality." This emphatic spirituality implies pastoral counselors' intimacy relationship with counselees. Pastoral counselors' psychological understandings about male mid-life crisis are theoretical frameworks to understand counselees, whereas pastoral counselors' mature faith is about self-discipline. And this **emphatic spirituality in terms of vertical dimension** means the tool, integrating the two categories for the practical application of the theories and the self-discipline. This emphatic spirituality requires an interpersonal dynamic relationship which is the most crucial thing between pastoral counselors and counselees. Surely, counselees bring their own personal problems with the expectation of solving them through pastoral counseling. But, simultaneously, another emerging problem of counselees is that they want to know what personal problems they must disclose to pastoral counselors. The secure and positive answer regarding this question can formulate an optimistic interpersonal dynamic relationship between pastoral counselors and counselees, and this interpersonal dynamic relation affects to bring out the positive result of pastoral counseling. Pastoral counselor and psychotherapist Chris Schilauch mentions the importance of this interpersonal dynamic relationship as follows:

> ...what is healing may be "caught more than taught." Care and cure have less to do with theory, technique, interpretation, insight,

metapsychology or theory than with the theoretician, technician, interpreter, seer, metapsychologist or theologian. It is the *person* and the *relationship* which shape and enable to process of healing.[37]

In other words, although pastoral counselors have prominent psychological understanding and practice the self-discipline for vertical dimensions, if they cannot formulate this interpersonal dynamic relationship, they cannot expect effective results of pastoral counseling, because they fail to formulate a "trust relationship." Thus, pastoral counselors need this *emphatic spirituality* to keep sustaining the interpersonal dynamic with counselees. *Emphatic spirituality* in pastoral counseling means to tune counselors' minds to the same feelings and thoughts of counselees. In other words, it means folding pastoral counselors' prejudice and preunderstanding and getting into the inner world of counselees. According to etymological research, empathy means to know others' abilities in terms of getting into their shoes.[38] Heinz Kohut emphasizes three reasons why empathy is inevitable in psychotherapy. First, empathy can be a good tool for observing counselees' psychological situations. He believes that without empathy human life will remain unintelligible. In the case of pastoral counseling, also, empathy, which is a tool for observe counselees' faith, can increase the effectiveness of counseling.[39] Secondly, empathy formulates a powerful psychological attachment, which brings out a positive result of counseling, between counselors and counselees in terms of expanding the self of counselors toward counselees. Thirdly, empathy is psychological nutrient and human life cannot be sustained without it, because empathy is "accepting, confirming and understanding human echoes evoked by the self." Furthermore, empathy is as indispensable to human beings as oxygen.[40] In other words, what we can learn from the definition of empathy through Heinz Kohut is that it is the most foundational element for counseling. In this sense, empathy is essential not only in counseling but also in human relationships. And then, how can this empathy can be related to the attitudes of pastoral counselors during counseling? Margaret Guenther insists that it active listening is important in pastoral counseling and ministry. I think that this empathetic mind in pastoral counseling can appear as active listening. By experiencing active listening as the opened mind of pastoral counselors, counselees begin to disclose themselves.[41] In fact, we are not accustomed to listening to someone, because we have not been educated at all on how to listen, but to speak. Thus, listening to someone who has sufferings is a real labor of love. Without love this labor of pastoral counseling cannot be accomplished. True and active listening is a total manifestation of love.[42] Every story spoken by counselees has some hidden meanings. Thus, pastoral counselors need to find out the real meaning of the story. This hidden meaning has some symbolic level. To figure out this hidden meaning the pastoral counselors need to be discerning and make counselees open their hearts.[43] This active listening can open counselees' minds and can assess the hidden meanings of stories spoken by counselees.[44] In a theological perspective, as we listen to counselees' contexts, we can listen to God. The relationship between pastoral counselors and counselees shows the pastoral counselors' relationship with God. So the decline of spiritual life begins when pastoral counselors do not listen actively to the sufferings of counselees. Active listening reflects the pastoral counselor's attitude, who is engaged in counseling with empathy. From a pastoral theological standpoint, Chris Schlauch defines empathy as follows:

> ...I suggest the metaethical, religious statement that we should relate empathically because we are created by God to do so, and raise the expressly theological statement that our capacity and responsibility to act empathically reflects our being made in the image of God. The empathic stance, as style of care, is an expression of the Imago of Dei.[45]

As Schlauch explains the meaning of empathy, he indicates that empathy is a pertinent term which can describe God's image formulated in human beings. As it were, empathy is the exactly expressed term which can show God's love and care through Jesus Christ.[46]

As we experience the encounter of the Spirit, we begin the journey of generative men whose characteristics are caring for others, community concerns, providing and educating future generations, etc. Regarding the virtue of generativity, Erikson mentions that "care" is the virtue of the seventh stage of his psychosocial theory. And Schlauch indicates that empathy is the style of care. Based on it we can say that generative men's minds are filled with empathic spirituality. Theologically speaking, a "new being" is a being who is transformed from apathy to empathy. "Empathic spirituality" is the representative tendency of the image of God. In a word, generativity means the recovered image of God in human beings.

It is impossible to experience intimacy without experiencing and having empathic spirituality. The power of empathy brings out therapeutic milieus because it can make us participate in others and accept and understand others as they are.[47] Thus, in pastoral counseling, pastoral counselors have to have empathic spirituality through which they can have interpersonal dynamic relations with counselees. By this experience pastoral counselors can understand and know how to help male mid-lifers to participate in the process of generative men.

Church as Caring Community

Up to the present, I have explained pastoral counselors' prerequisites as ways of pastoral interventions. Now I want to suggest how the church can provide necessary pastoral interventions as a caring community for male mid-lifers. The concept of caring community reminds us of Erikson's concept of "cogwheeling of life." Because a person has an interactive relationship his social milieu, a supportive caring community as church is inevitable for the best result of male mid-life crisis. First of all, psychologically speaking, Heinz Kohut mentions that even healthy-mind persons need objects which can be mirrors for them. As it were, even mature persons need idealized objects for their psychological development. This idealization is very healthy, and it can support and help people to take an incessant process of transformation.[48] Applying this concept of idealization to pastoral interventions, male mid-lifers need objects which can be idealizations for their psychological, physical, and spiritual wholeness. In others words, in pastoral intervention perspectives, the church needs to provide and teach about objects which can be spiritual models and mentors, whose lives can help and challenge male mid-lifers. What I want to suggest for objects for idealization are the lives of Jesus and saints. The church needs to provide and educate how and why their lives were meaningful. Through idealization about them, male mid-lifers can take and imitate the process of transformation in order to be generative men. What we can be sure of is that as we are absorbed in imitating the life of Jesus and the generative lives of saints, male mid-lifers can be challenged to take the transformation process of generative men.[49] Through this process of idealization male mid-lifers can receive helpful instructions for their mid-life crisis. In pastoral perspective for male mid-lifers, what is important is to provide some milieu in which they may experience the awareness of God and help them to respond appropriately to God, because they will not lose the directions for male mid-life crisis in terms of idealization of lives of Jesus and saints.[50] Not only for this reason but also for male mid-lifers we need a supportive caring community such as a church to encourage our male mid-lifers. Secondly, the church needs to prepare the school for male mid-lifers. Even Jung indicates the necessity of school for adults who are in mid-life. Through the school for adults we need to teach male mid-lifers about what they have to focus on in their second half of life without wasting their time. Most male mid-lifers are not educated about the second half of life because most educational institutions, from elementary schools through graduate schools, educate them how could they be functional persons in organizations. Even today most of us have been educated as to how we can we fit into social organizations and institutions. Because of this phenomenon, most adults have rarely been educated about mid-life identity/crisis in spiritual perspectives. In this point of view, if the church can provide the education for male mid-lifers about the spiritual meaning of mid-life and mid-life identity, etc., so many male mid-lifers can have a chance to take the process of generative men for the true meaning of their lives.

A case story about an eighty-year-old man informs the urgency of educational plans of the church for mid-lifers. This man had medical treatments for his serious stomach cancer as an advanced age of 80 when a counselor visited him. What he confessed to the counselor at the last stage of his stomach cancer was about his son-in-law and a daughter. He always had thought about the son-in-law and the daughter as persons who had never succeeded in society. His son-in-law and daughter were in charge of missionary work, such as helping and counseling for those who were in need of help. Because of their roles and jobs, the father-in-law usually had complained about them; "How can you say that you work for suffering neighbors and community without providing enough material for your family?" Whenever he blamed and criticized them they talked to him as follows; "This is meaningful and we feel happiness as we do our jobs. And this is what we want to do." As father heard about their response he thought that they were crazy. "But now I think that they live the most meaningful life. I realize about the meaningful live not until I face death because of cancer. But they know what is valuable and meaningful in their lives, for they have never complained and regretted their missionary work." After leaving this message he died at the age of

80 because of cancer. This story makes us reflect to compare a generative man with a self-absorptive man, and assists us in realizing the urgency of school/education/plans of the church for mid-lifers. Through these we can provide and teach the meaning of the second half of life and prepare generative men for their meaningful and valuable lives. It is too late to realize the meaning of life in spiritual perspective at the moment of dying. In this sense what I mean when I say that we need the adults' school for mid-lifers does not only mean education for preparing mid-lifers but also the need for generative mentors/teachers who have experienced mid-life crisis. Through the relationship with generative mentors, male mid-lifers will have challenges to take a process of generative men. Generative mentors' life experience, faith journey, etc., can inspire and encourage mid-lifers to participate in the journey of generative men. The more the church provides the school and generative mentors for the journey of male mid-lifers, the more we will experience generative family, community and society. But this education in the church does not mean a temporary school, it should be a life-term education. And this education in the church needs to provide not only mid-lifers but also young adults. By being concerned for young adults, we can give them a map traveled before they face the mid-life identity, and they can have more time to reflect about generative men. As the church and pastoral counselors provide pastoral caring and milieus for male mid-lifers, we will experience the result of it as the responsible self, the believable self, and the accessible self who can renew the relationship with oneself, others and God in terms of recovering the centered self.

Summary

According to scholars 80 percent of male mid-lifers have experienced mid-life crisis, male mid-life crisis is regarded as a general phenomenon. As I did psychological and theological research regarding the cause of male mid-life crisis, I can say that the most crucial cause of male mid-life crisis comes from the loss of the centered self as the archetypal image of God. The loss of the centered self has been expressed as stagnation at mid-life. Regarding stagnation at mid-life Donald Capps divides it into two categories: passive stagnation as the absence of hope and desire, and active stagnation as distortion of hope.[51]

The results of stagnation can be expressed as the destructive relationship of oneself, others, and God. Thus the crisis of male mid-life implies a spiritual crisis in contemporary society. Regarding the healing for mid-life crisis, Donald Capps suggests that the purpose of pastoral care is to reconstruct and foster the self in the perspective of hope for responsible self, believable self, and accessible self which implies the image of God. But the possibility of recovering the self is only possible in terms of "replacing oneself as the center of one's existence with God.[52] In order to experience this Capps mentions that we need to be open (conversion) always toward God. Regarding the conversion experience Raymond Studzinski indicates that it is crucial in order to experience the recovering of the centered self, because conversion means to have a new relationship with onself, others and God.[53] In the same vein Capps regards that the real transformation at mid-life can happen in terms of encountering the Eternal Self, God.

For effective pastoral counseling, pastoral counselors need to prepare themselves to understand three things: God, the person, and the relationship between counselors and counselees. In other word, first, psychological understanding about male mid-life is necessary, because it not only provides counselors with psychological knowledge but also it can help pastoral counselors analyze the relation of God to them. Secondly, pastoral counselors need pertinent faith, vertical dimension, for pastoral counseling. Without it pastoral counselees cannot formulate therapeutic and safe milieu to counselees. Thirdly, pastoral counselors need to have "emphatic spirituality" which implies a horizontal dimension with counselees. In this same vein, Heinz Kohut emphasizes the important role of empathy in psychotherapy. Lastly, the church as caring community needs to take a role in order to provide the education for mid-lifers.

The more we have male mid-lifers who have started the process of becoming generative men, the more we will experience a generative community through which our children will learn justice, peace, and love. In terms of generative people who are parts of family, society, and the world, we will experience the silent revolution which persists until it accomplishes the mission for human worlds. For this mission, generative community, we all need to take on the process of generative men. It is not facile. But we need to do it for family, society, and global community. As we take this process to encounter the archetypal image of God as the centered self at mid-life, we will feel more the meaning of our lives through ourselves, others, and God because we will experience the transformation of ourselves by opening ourselves toward God.

(Notes)

1. Donald Capps, "Pastoral Counseling for Middle Adults" in *Clinical Handbook of Pastoral Counseling*, Vol. 1. eds. Robert J. Wicks, Richard D. Parsons, and Donald Capps (New York and Manwah: Paulist Press, 1993), 241.
2. Ibid.
3. Ibid.
4. Ibid., 240.
5. William A. Barry, "Spiritual Direction and Pastoral Counseling," *Pastoral Psychology* 26:1 (Fall 1977): 5.
6. Howard Clinebell, *Basic Types of Pastoral Care and Counseling: Resources for the Ministry of Healing and Growth* (Nashville: Abingdon Press, 1984), 108.
7. John J. Shea, "Adult Faith, Pastoral Counseling, and Spiritual Direction," *The Journal of Pastoral Care*, 51:3 (Fall 1997): 259.
8. Ibid., 266.
9. Donald Capps, *Deadly Sins and Saving Virtues* (Philadelphia: Fortress Press, 1987), 63.
10. Henri J. M. Nouwen, *With Open Hands* (Notre Dame, Indiana: Ave Maria Press, 1982), 57.
11. Raymond Studzinski, *Spiritual Direction and Midlife Development* (Chicago: Loyola University Press, 1985), 3. Not only Raymond Studzinski but also Daniel Levinson in his book *The Seasons of a Man's Life* points out that male mid-life identity/crisis has happened through all times and places.
12. Ibid., 61.
13. Walter E. Conn, "Adult Conversion," *Pastoral Psychology* 34:4 (Summer 1986): 225.
14. Donald Capps, "Sin, Narcissism, and the Changing Face of Narcissism," *Journal of Religion and Health* 29: 3 (Fall 1990): 233-234.
15. James Fowler, *Becoming Adult, Becoming Christian: Adult Development and Christian Faith* (New York: HarperSanFrancisco, 1984), 140.
16. *ST.* Vol. 1, 49.
17. Paul Tillich, "Theology and Counseling," in *The Meaning of Health: Essays in Existentialism, Psychoanalysis and Religion*, 119.
18. Viktor Frankle, *The Doctor and the Soul: An Introduction to Logotherapy* (New York: Knof, 1973), 9.
19. Kevin G. Culligan, "The Counseling Ministry and Spiritual Dimension," in *Pastoral Counseling*, eds. Barry K. Estadt, Melvin C, Blanchette, and John R. Compton (New Jersey: Prentice Hall, 1991), 9.
20. William A. Barry, op. cit., 2, 6.
21. Theron S. Nease, "Pastoral Care: generativity or Stagnation?" *Pastoral Psychology* 26:4 (Summer 1978): 256.

22. William Barry, op. cit., 4.
23. Kenneth Leech, *Spirituality and Pastoral Care* (Mass: Cowley, 1989), 48.
24. Kevin Culligan, op. cit., 37.
25. Kenneth Leech, *Soul Friend: The Practice of Christian Spirituality* (San Francisco: Harper Collins, 1992), 104-05.
26. Kevin Culligan, op. cit., 45.
27. Ibid., 44.
28. Paul W. Pruyer, *The Minister As Diagnostician: Personal Problem in Pastoral Perspective* (Philadelphia: The Westminster Press, 1976), 49-50.
29. Kevin Culligan, op. cit., 9.
30. John J. Shea, op. cit., 268.
31. Ibid.
32. Kenneth Leech, *Spirituality and Pastoral Care*, 36.
33. Ibid., 79.
34. Paul Tillich, "Theology and Counseling," in *The Meaning of Health: Essays in Existentialism, Psychoanalysis and Religion*, 119.
35. Charles A. Curran, *Religious Values in Counseling & Psychotherapy* (New York: Sheed and Ward, 1969), 280-81.
36. Joseph D. Driskill, " Pastoral Counseling and Spiritual Direction: Enrichment Where the Twain Meet," in *Pastoral Psychology* 41:4 (1993): 221.
37. Chris Schilauch, "Empathy as the Essence of Pastoral Psychotherapy," *The Journal of Pastoral Care* XLIV:1 (Spring 1990): 3.
38. Ibid.
39. John Sheal, op. cit., 259.
40. Heinz Kohut, "The Psychoanalyst in the Community of Scholars," in *The Search for the Self*, ed. Paul Ornsten (New York: International Universities Press, 1978), 705.
41. Margaret Guenther, *Holy Listening: The Art of Spiritual Direction* (Cambridge, Boston: Cowley Publications, 1992), 37-40.
42. Scott Peck, *The Roadless Traveled: A New Psychology of Love, Traditional Values and Spiritual Growth* (New York: Touchstone, 1978), 129.
43. Margaret Guenther, op, cit., 87.
44. Donald Peel, *The Ministry of Listening* (Toronto, Canada: Anglican Book Center, 1980), 33.
45. Chris Schlauch, op. cit., 16-17.
46. Ibid.
47. John Shea, op. cit. 265.
48. Heinz Kohut, *The Analysis of the Self* (New York: International Universities Press, 1971), 74-86.
49. Kevin Culligan, op. cit. 41.
50. Joseph D. Driskill, op. cit., 218.
51. Donald Capps, *Deadly Sins and Saving Virtues*, 61.
52. Donald Capps, *Pastoral Counseling for Middle Adults*, 241.
53. Raymond Stuzinski, op. cit., 61.

Biblography

Alkin, L.R.(1994). *Dying, Death, and Bereavement*. Boston: Allyn and Bacon.

Baruch, G. and Brooks-Gunn, J.(1984). *Women in Midlife*. New York: Plenum Press.

Barry, W. A.(1977). "Spiritual Direction and Pastoral Counseling," *Pastoral Psychology*. Vol. 26(1). Fall 4-11.

Becker, E.(1971). *The Birth and Death of Meaning*: An Interdisciplinary Perspective on the Problem of Man. New York: Free Press.

_____.(1973). *The Denial of Death*. New York: Free Press.

Bee, H. L.(1992). *The Journey of Adulthood*. New York: Macmillan Publishing Company.

Boerzoff, J. et al.(1996). *Inside Out and Outside In*. New Jersey/London: Janson Aronson Inc.

Brim, Jr. O. G.(1980). "Theories of the Male Mid-life Crisis" in *Counseling Adults*. eds., Nancy K. Schlossber and Alan D. Engine. California: Book/Cole Publishing Company.

Browning, D.(1973). *Generative Man: Psychoanalysis Perspectives*. Philadelphia: The Westminster Press.

_____.(1976). "Conference on Erikson and Religion" in *Criterion*. University of Chicago. Vol.1. Spring. 25-26.

Buber, M.(1967). *Between Man and Man*. New York: Macmillan.

Capps, D.(1987). *Deadly Sins and Saving Virtues*. Philadelphia: Fortress Press.

_____.(1990). "Sin, Narcissism, and the Changing Face of Conversion," *Journal of Religion and Health*, Vol. 28(3). Fall 1990. 233-251.

_____.(1993). "Pastoral Counseling for Middle Adults" in *Clinical Handbook of Pastoral Counseling*, Vol. 1 eds. Robert Wick, Richard D. Parsons, & Donald Capps. New York: Paulist Press.

Chapman, H. J.(1988). *Jung's Three Theories of Religious Experience*. Levinston/ Queenston: The Edwin Ellen Press.

Charet, F. X.(1933). *Spiritualism and the Foundations of C.G. Jung's Psychology*. Albany: State University of New York Press. .

Clift, W.B.(1994). *Jung and Christianity*. New York: Crossroad.

Chodorow, N.(1978). *The Reproduction of Mothering: Psychoanalysis and the Sociology of Gender*. Berkley: University of California.

_____.(1989). *Feminism and Psychoanalysis Theory*. New Haven: Yale University Press.

_____.(1994). *Feminities, Masculinities, Sexualities: Freud and Beyond*. Lexington. KY: University Press of Kentucky.

Clinebell, H.(1984). *Basic Types of Pastoral Care and Counseling: Resources for the Ministry of Healing and Growth*. Nashville: Abingdon Press.

Conn, W. E.(1986). "Adult Conversion" *Pastoral Psychology*. Vol. 34(4). summer. 225-236.

Culligan, K.(1991). "The Counseling Ministry and Spiritual Dimension." in *Pastoral Counseling*. eds. Barry K. Estadt, Melvin C. Blanchette, and John R. Compton. New Jersey: Prentice Hall.

Curran . C.(1969). *Religious Values in Counseling and Psychotherapy*. New York: Sheed and Ward.

Dourley, J. P.(1991). *The Psyche as Sacrament: A Comparative Study of C.G. Jung and Paul Tillich*. Toronto. Canada: Inner City Books. .

Dowing, C.(1987). *Journey Through Menopause: A Personal Rite of Passage*. New York: Crossroad.

Driskill, J. D.(1993). "Pastoral Counseling and Spiritual Direction: Enrichment Where the Twain Meet." *Pastoral Psychology*. Vol. 41: 4. 217-235.

Edinger, E. F.(1992). *Ego and Archetype: Individuation and the Religious Function of Psyche*, Boston & New York: Shambala.

Eliade, E.(1987). *The Sacred and the Profane: The Nature of Religion*. New York & London: Harvest Book Harcourt Barce.

_____.(1991). *The Myth of the Eternal Return: Cosmos and History*. New Jersey: Princeton University.

_____.(1985). " A New Humanism." in *Waiting for the Down: Mircea Eliade in Perspective*. Ed. Carrasco, D, Sanberg, J. Boulder & London: Westview Press.

_____.(1973). "The Sacred in the Secular World" in *Cultural Hermeutics* Vol. 1. ed. David M. Rasmussen. Dordrecht-Holland/Boston-USA: D. Reidel Publishing Company.

Erikson, E. H. "The Roots of Virtue" in *The Humanist Frame*. New York: Harper and Bros.

_____.(1963). *Childhood and Society*. New York & London: Norton.

_____.(1969). *Gandhi's Truth*. New York: Norton.

_____.(1969). *Identity: Youth and Crisis*. New York: Norton &

Company.

_____.(1980). *Identity and the Life Cycle*. New York & London: Norton.

_____.(1982). *The Life Cycle Completed*. New York: Norton & Company.

Erikson, E. H. and Erikson, Joan M.(1981). *On Generativity and Identity: From a Conversation with Erik and Joan Erikson*. Harvard Educational Review. Vol.51(2). 269.

Erikson, E. H., et.al.(1985). *Vital Involvement in Old Age: The Experience of Old Age in Our Time*. New York and London: Norton.

Feifel, H.(1965). *The Meaning of Death*. New York: McGraw-Hill Book Company.

Fiske, M.(1979). *Middle Age*. New York: Harper & Row.

Fowler, J. (1984). *Becoming Adult, Becoming Christian: Adult Development and Christian Faith*. New York: HarperSanFrancisco.

Frankle, V.(1973). *The Doctor and the Soul: An Introduction to Logotherapy*. New York: Knof.

Freud. S.(1989). *Leonardo da Vinci and a Memory of His Childhood*. New York: Norton.

Fuller, R. C.(1988). *Religion and Life Cycle*. Philadelphia: Fortress Press.

Gilligan, C.(1982). *In a Different Voice*. Cambridge: Harvard University.

Gleitman, H.(1987). *Basic Psychology*. New York/London: Norton Company.

Gorman, M.(1993). "Midlife Transition in Men and Women," in

Clinical Handbook of Pastoral Counseling. Vol 2. eds. Robert J. Wicks and Richard D. Parsons. New York and Manwah: Paulist Book.

Guenther, M.(1992). *Holy Listening*. Cambridge, Boston: Cowley Publications.

Gutmann, D.(1994). *Reclaimed Powers: Men and Women in Later Life*. Evanston. Illinois: Northwestern University.

_____.(1997). *The Human Elder in Nature, Culture & Society*. Boulder. Colorado: West View Press.

Hall, E.(1983). "A Conversation with Erik Erikson" in *Psychology Today*. (June1983).

Hall, J. & Young-Elsendrath.P.(1991). *Jung's Self Psychology: A Constructivist Perspective*. New York & London: The Guilford Press.

Homans, P.(1995). *Jung in Context*. Chicago: University of Chicago.

Hunter, R.(1990).(ed). *Dictionary of Pastoral Care and Counseling*. Nashville: Abingdon Press.

Jaques, E.(1965). "The Mid-life Crisis and Death" in International Journal of Psychoanalysis Vol. 46. 502-515.

_____.(1981). "Midlife Crisis" in *The Course of Life* (Vol. 3)*: Adulthood and the Aging Process*. eds. Greenspan, S. & Pollock, G. Maryland: National Institute of Mental Health.

_____.(1985). "The Midlife Crisis" in *Forty* .ed. Stanley Brandes. Knoxville: The University of Tennessee Press.

Jones, J. W.(1991). *Contemporary Psychoanalysis and Religion*. New Haven: Yale University Press.

Jung, C. G.(1933). *Modern Man in Search of A Soul*, trans. W. S. Dell and Cary F. Baynes. New York: Harcourt Brace Jovanovich.

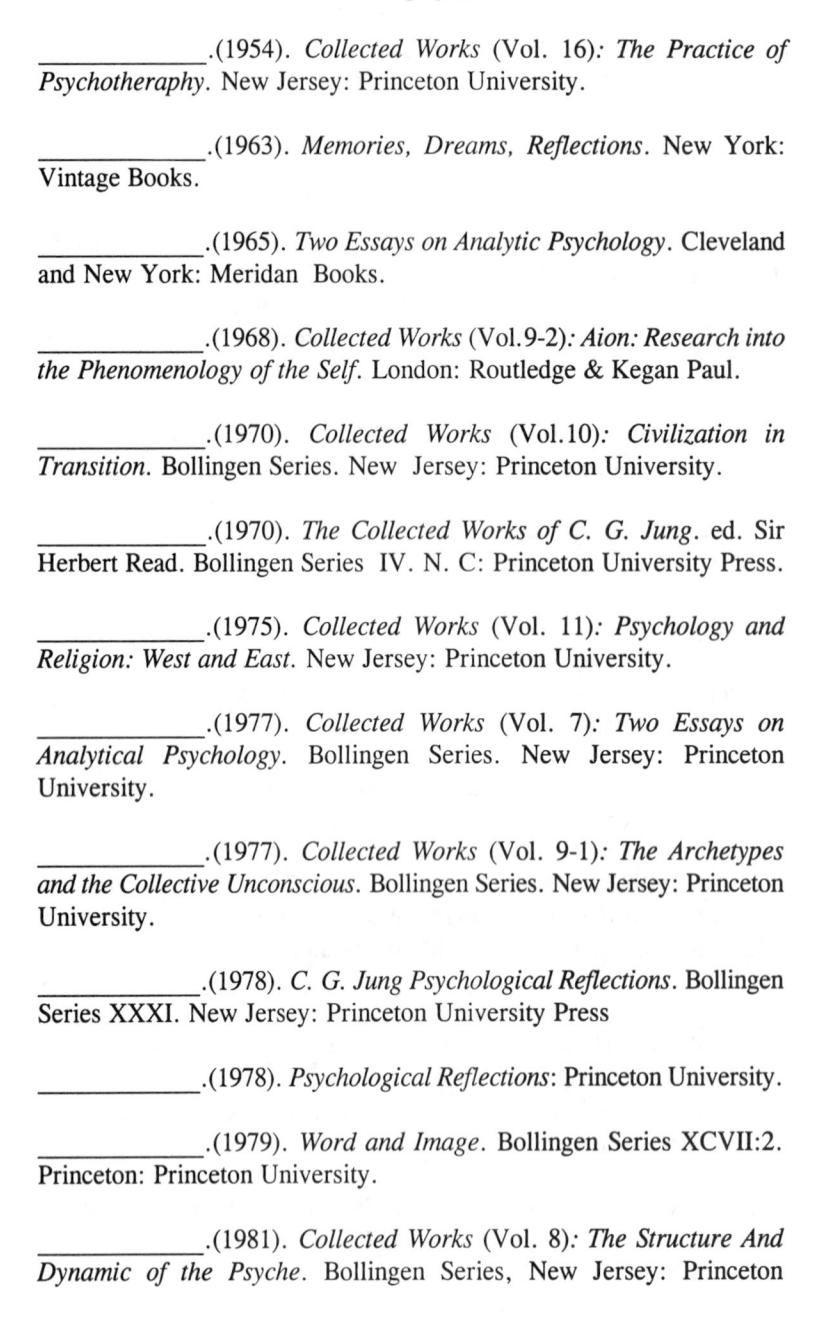

_____.(1954). *Collected Works* (Vol. 16): *The Practice of Psychotheraphy*. New Jersey: Princeton University.

_____.(1963). *Memories, Dreams, Reflections*. New York: Vintage Books.

_____.(1965). *Two Essays on Analytic Psychology*. Cleveland and New York: Meridan Books.

_____.(1968). *Collected Works* (Vol.9-2): *Aion: Research into the Phenomenology of the Self*. London: Routledge & Kegan Paul.

_____.(1970). *Collected Works* (Vol.10): *Civilization in Transition*. Bollingen Series. New Jersey: Princeton University.

_____.(1970). *The Collected Works of C. G. Jung*. ed. Sir Herbert Read. Bollingen Series IV. N. C: Princeton University Press.

_____.(1975). *Collected Works* (Vol. 11): *Psychology and Religion: West and East*. New Jersey: Princeton University.

_____.(1977). *Collected Works* (Vol. 7): *Two Essays on Analytical Psychology*. Bollingen Series. New Jersey: Princeton University.

_____.(1977). *Collected Works* (Vol. 9-1): *The Archetypes and the Collective Unconscious*. Bollingen Series. New Jersey: Princeton University.

_____.(1978). *C. G. Jung Psychological Reflections*. Bollingen Series XXXI. New Jersey: Princeton University Press

_____.(1978). *Psychological Reflections*: Princeton University.

_____.(1979). *Word and Image*. Bollingen Series XCVII:2. Princeton: Princeton University.

_____.(1981). *Collected Works* (Vol. 8): *The Structure And Dynamic of the Psyche*. Bollingen Series, New Jersey: Princeton

University.

_____.(1981). *Collected Works* (Vol. 17*): The Development of Personality*. New Jersey, Princeton University.

Kagan, J. and Havemann, E.(1980). *Psychology*. New York: Harcourt Brace Jovanovich Inc.

Kohut, H.(1971). *The Analysis of the Self*. New York: International Universities Press.

_____.(1978). "The Psychoanalysist in the Community of Scholars" in *The Search of the Self*. New York: International Universities Press.

Korte, J.(1984). *Outliving the Self: Generativity and the Interpretation of Lives*. Baltimore and London: The Johns Hopkins University Press.

Lachman, M. E. and Boone J. J. (1997). *Multiple Paths of Midlife Development*. Chicago: The University of Chicago Press.

Lake, A.(1979). *Our Own Years*. New York: Random House Book.

Leech, K.(1989). *Pastoral Care and Spirituality*. Mass: Cowley Publication.

_____.(1992). *Soul Friend*. San Francisco: Harper Collins.

Levinson, D. J.(1978). *The Seasons of a Man's Life*. New York: Ballantine Books.

Lifton, R. J.(1974). "The Sense of Immortality: One Death and the Continuity of Life," in *Exploration and Psychohistory*. New York: Simon and Schuster.

Lindzey, G. and Hall, Calvin S. (1959).*Theories of Personality*. New York: John Wiley & Sons.

Matton, M. A.(1981). *Jungian Psychology in Perspective*. New York & London: Free Press.

McAdams, D. P.(1993). *The Stories We Live By: Personal Myths and the Making of the Self*. New York: William Morrow and Company.

_____.(1994). *The Person: An Introduction to Personality Psychology*. Orlando: Harcourt Brace Collage Publishers.

McKelway, A. J.(1964). *The Systematic Theology of Paul Tillich*. New York: A Delta Book.

Miller, J. B.(1973). *Psychoanalysis and Women*. New York: Brunner/Mazel Publishers.

Moore, R & Gillette. D.(1990). *King, Warrior, Magician, Lover: Rediscovering the Archetypes of the Mature Masculine*. New York: HaperSanFrancisco..

_____.(1990). *Jung and Christianity in Dialogue: Faith, Feminism and Hermeutics*. New York: Paulist Press.

_____.(1992). *The King Within: Accessing the King in the Male Psyche*. New York. William Morrow and Company Inc.

Moore, R.(1984). "Space and Transformation in Human Experience" in *Anthropology and the Study of Religion*. Chicago: Center for the Scientific Study of Religion.

Nagy, M.(1991). *Philosophical Issues in the Psychology of C.G. Jung*. Ablany: State University of New York Press.

Nease, T. S.(1978). "Pastoral Care: Generativity or Stagnation?" *Pastoral Psychology*. Vol.26(4). Summer. 253-262.

Neugarten, B. L.(1967), "The Awareness of Middle Age." in *Middle Age*.(ed. Owen, Roger). London:British Broadcasting Corporation.

Newman, B. M.(1982). "Midlife Development."in *Handbook of Developmental Psychology*, ed. Benjamin B. Wolman. New Jersey: Prentice Hall.

Nouwen, H. J. M. (1982).*With Open Hand*. Notre Dame Indiana: Ave Maria Press.

Pannenberg, W.(1976). *Theology and the Philosophy of Science*. Philadelphia: The Westminster Press.

_____.(1985). *Anthropology in Theological Perspective*. Philadelphia: The Westminster Press.

Panek, P.E and Hayslip, B.(1993). *Adult Development and Aging*: Harper Collins College Publishers.

Peck, S.(1978). *The Roadless Traveled: A New Psychology of Love, Traditional Values and Spiritual Growth*. New York: Touchstone.

Perlmutter, M. and Hall E.(1983): *Adult Development and Aging*. New York: John Wiley & Sons.

Phipps, W. E.(1985). *Death: Confronting the Reality*. Atlanta: John Knox Press.

Pruyer, P.(1976). *The Minister As Diagnostician: Personal Problem in Pastoral Perspective*. Philadelphia: The Westminster Press.

Rennie, B.(1996). *Reconstructing Eliade: Making Sense of Religion*. New York: State University of New York Press.

Schar, H.(1950). *Religion and the Cure of Souls in Jung's Psychology.trans*. R.F.C. Hull. Bollingen Series 21. Pantheon Books.

Schilauch. C.(1990). "Empathy as the Essence of Pastoral Psychotherapy." *The Journal of Pastoral Care*. XLIV:1. Spring. 3-17.

Shea, J. J.(1997). "Adult Faith, Pastoral Counseling and Spiritual Direction." *The Journal of Pastoral Care*. 51: 3. 259-270.

Sheehy, G.(1995). *New Passages: Mapping Your Life Across Time*. New York: Random House.

Siegel, A. M.(1996). *Heinz Kohut and the Psychology of the Self.* London and New York: Routledge.

Singer, J.(1972). *Boundaries of the Soul.* New York: Anchor Books.

Smith, C. D.(1990). *Jung's Quest for Wholeness.* Albany: State University of New York Press.

Smith, M.(1995). *Psychotherapy and the Sacred.* Chicago: Center for the Scientific Study of Religion.

Stein, M.(1983). *In Midlife: A Jungian Perspective.* Dallas Texas: Spring Publication.

Stevens, A.(1990). *On Jung.* England: Penguin Books.

Strouse, J.(Ed.).(1974). *Women & Analysis.* New York: Grossman Publishers.

Studzinki, R.(1985). *Spiritual Direction and Midlife Development.* Chicago: Loyola University Press.

Sze, W.C.(1975). *Human Life Cycle.* New York: Jason Aronson.

Tillich, P.(1948). *The Shaking of the Foundation.* New York: Charles Scriber's Sons.

_____.(1951). *Systematic Theology* (Vol. 1). Chicago: University of Chicago.

_____.(1952). *The Courage To Be.* New Haven and London: Yale University Press.

_____.(1953). *The Protestant Era* (trans. Adams, James Luther). Chicago: University of Chicago.

_____.(1954). *Love Power and Justice: Ontological Analyses and Ethical Applications.* London. New York: Oxford University Press.

_____.(1955). *Biblical Religion and the Search for Ultimate Reality*. Chicago: University of Chicago.

_____.(1956). *The Religious Situation*. New York: Living Age Books.

_____.(1957). *Systematic Theology* (Vol. 2). Chicago: University of Chicago.

_____.(1957). *Dynamics of Faith*. New York: Harper & Brothers.

_____.(1959). *Theology of Culture* (ed. Kimball, Robert). London. New York: Oxford University.

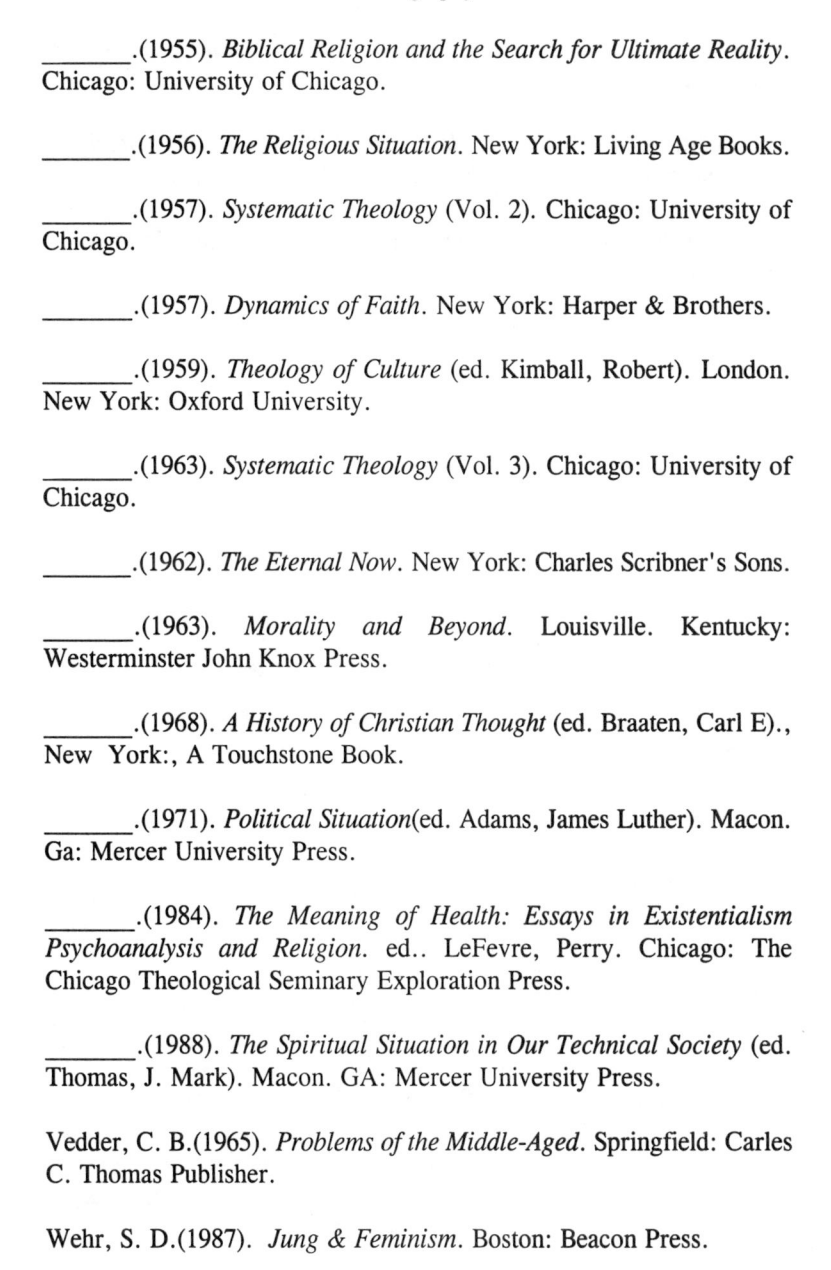

_____.(1963). *Systematic Theology* (Vol. 3). Chicago: University of Chicago.

_____.(1962). *The Eternal Now*. New York: Charles Scribner's Sons.

_____.(1963). *Morality and Beyond*. Louisville. Kentucky: Westerminster John Knox Press.

_____.(1968). *A History of Christian Thought* (ed. Braaten, Carl E)., New York:, A Touchstone Book.

_____.(1971). *Political Situation*(ed. Adams, James Luther). Macon. Ga: Mercer University Press.

_____.(1984). *The Meaning of Health: Essays in Existentialism Psychoanalysis and Religion*. ed.. LeFevre, Perry. Chicago: The Chicago Theological Seminary Exploration Press.

_____.(1988). *The Spiritual Situation in Our Technical Society* (ed. Thomas, J. Mark). Macon. GA: Mercer University Press.

Vedder, C. B.(1965). *Problems of the Middle-Aged*. Springfield: Carles C. Thomas Publisher.

Wehr, S. D.(1987). *Jung & Feminism*. Boston: Beacon Press.

Williams, J. H.(1977). *Psychology of Women*. New York: W. W. Norton & Company.

Winnicott. D. W.(1996). *The Maturational Process and the Facilitating Environment*. Connecticut: International Universities Press.

Wulff, D. M.(1991). *Psychology of Religion*. New York: John Wiley & Sons.

ABOUT THE AUTHOR

Justin K. Lim was born in 1959 and is a graduate of Seoul Theological University. He trained for his theological studies at Garrett Evangelical-Theological Seminary(M. Div, 1993; MTS, 1996) and graduated from the Chicago Theological Seminary in the field of Pastoral Psychology and Pastoral Theology (Ph. D.) He did interdisciplinary studies in psychology and human development theories at the University of Chicago and Northwestern University. Currently, he is a local pastor in Chicago. His e-mail address is Kyungslim@hotmail.com.